Communication,

Sex and Money

by
Edwin Louis Cole

Honor Books
Tulsa, OK 74155

Unless otherwise indicated, all Scripture quotations are taken from the *King James Version* of the Bible.

17th Printing
Over 212,000 in Print

Communication, Sex and Money
ISBN 1-56292-474-5
Copyright © 1987 by Edwin Louis Cole
International Headquarters
P. O. Box 610588
Dallas, TX 75261

Published by Honor Books
P. O. Box 55388
Tulsa, Oklahoma 74155

CONTENTS

Dedicated to the
"loveliest lady in the land,"
my wife Nancy.

INTRODUCTION

We live in a day of blended families, delinquent dads, women's lib, latchkey kids, role conditioning, genetic engineering, designer drugs, lost milk-carton children, passive papas and microwave Christianity. It's a mixed-up world.

Compromise is the rule of the day. Our society deals with images, not issues. We suffer from the recompense of having leaders who have great personal charisma but who seem totally devoid of upright character.

It's a day when a national news anchorperson says, "The mass media is creating a market for mediocrity." It is a time when perversion of truth and principles occurs with impunity. It is an hour when the world stands in need of men, but gets wimps.

What the world cannot control, it decriminalizes and legalizes. What Christianity cannot control, it psychologizes and rationalizes.

Today 130,000 high school students openly admit to being "stoned" every day, and there are 1,000,000 runaway children on the streets with a median age of fifteen. Seventy percent of them are white, and twenty percent are black.

In a poll of 469 pastors across the nation, sixty percent said fornication is acceptable, ninety percent said there should be no legal sanctions against extramarital sex, and seventy percent agreed that homosexuality is not sufficient cause to refuse ordination into the ministry.

Single-parent homes have doubled in fifteen years, until today roughly a quarter of all U.S. homes are single-parented, and over ninety percent of all single-parent homes are parented by a woman.

In the most prosperous nation on earth, suicide is becoming widespread as the leading cause of death among the young, and lauded as a respectable form of death among the old.

In one state alone (California), over 400,000 women receive aid for dependent children because the fathers of the children have abandoned their families.

It is a time of perverted peculiarity when some of the same people who protest the death penalty in our prisons also parade in favor of abortion.

Language has been semanticized until permissiveness, passivity and pacification are often simply euphemistic terms for cowardice.

Sperm banks, surrogate motherhood, Hollywood glamorization of the spirit of whoredoms, porno queens, herpes, AIDS, and condoms — not continence — are normal in an abnormal society.

Greenmail is now joined to blackmail. Arbitrage has become the formal name for "insider trading," or cheating, in the stock market.

It's a time for men to come forward and be men.

Our world must have them, women anxiously seek them, children desperately need them, we cannot live without them.

The only thing women want men to be is men. And the only thing most men desire to be is men.

However, most men do not understand what it is to be a man. Books written today tell that real men don't eat quiche, but the truth is that real men, secure in their manhood, can eat anything they desire.

The answer is not to return to reruns of western movies and war films to bring back the spirit of *machismo*.

Conversion is necessary to rectify perversion.

Men today need the truth about manhood.

Truth is life's most priceless commodity.

A man in Florida wrote to me and said, "All my life I have wanted to be a man. I retired from the armed forces after thirty years, I've been married twenty-eight years, and in all this time no one has ever taught me what it is to be a man.

"Your book changed my life," he said. "For the first time in my life I understood what a real man was, and how I could be that man. Thank you."

That's reason enough for me to write this new book.

There are truths today that, as a man, you need to know.

It is the truth that will set you free to be the man God created you to be. Truth must be spoken in love. Love is the qualification for speaking the truth.

In preparing this book, we had a survey done of the letters received in our office, and with one exception the major concerns of every letter were basically about communication, sex and money.

The one exception was the overriding concern people had for the welfare of their friends and neighbors in a mixed-up world. It was the overwhelming desire of all who wrote to know that their loved ones were in a right relationship with God.

The survey showed other concerns to be: broken marriages, divine guidance in daily living, and drugs.

Many men who wrote expressed fear of their relationships with women, and many women — especially married women — confessed they had never experienced true love.

The common complaint of all women who wrote that their marriage was unsatisfactory was simply their husbands' failure to communicate. According to these ladies, lack of communication is the single most important failure of men.

Even the single women found it hard to establish communication with men. They complained that men do not know how to be friends, carry on an adult conversation, or understand what it means to be a gentleman.

However, for every problem created, God the Creator has a solution.

There are three basic problem areas in any relationship between a man and a woman. They are communication, sex and money. That is true whether the people are single or married.

In this mixed-up world, there are some basic truths that can help you in all three areas.

It is my prayer that the next few pages will begin to help change your life.

1
MAN: THE GLORY OF GOD

Fame can come in a moment, but greatness comes with longevity.

Men were created for greatness.

In fact, they were created for more than greatness; they were created for the glory of God.

The last seven years of my life have been spent with men, watching a "new awakening" take place in hundreds of thousands of men's lives throughout the world, as they came to an understanding of what it is to be the man they were created to be.

And — I've heard the humor applied to it.

At a men's conference, Leonard Albert, the master of ceremonies, introduced me as the speaker to a throng of men with these words: "Last year when Mr. Cole was here, one of the men became so excited about becoming a 'maximized man' that he went home immediately to tell his wife what kind of man he was going to be, and how she needed to respond to it.

"She didn't receive it the way he thought she would and the exchange between them became so heated that it did not cool off until he finally got her down on her knees. There she was, on her knees, in the bedroom, looking under the bed, and saying, 'Come out and fight like a man!' "

The same place where Leonard shared his humor another fellow told this:

"Adam was standing with his two sons on the riverbank looking back across at Eden from whence they had come, and while staring at it he told them, 'Sons, that's where we used to live before Mother ate us out of house and home.' "

We can joke all we want to, but the truth is — life is not a joke nor are relationships a joking matter.

With many, marriage can be the closest thing to a heaven or hell they will ever have in this life.

As men, we need to understand that God made men and women unique, to be different from all other creatures — and from each other.

They were, and are, created to fulfill different purposes and roles in life.

However, it is these very differences between them that cause difficulties in maintaining their relationship together.

The differences were meant to bring balance and blessing to human lives, not to disrupt, disturb, demean, or destroy them.

God created man in His image and for His glory, and created the woman for the glory of the man.

In the scriptural account of creation it shows Adam to be "alone." Being "alone" can be a blessing, but being "lonely" never is. His aloneness degenerated into loneliness and became a cursing rather than a blessing.

In Eden, Adam had fellowship with God, but he had no peer because God is without peer.

Adam loved God, but he was still without an object of his love on earth that was his peer. For love to be love, there must be an object of love.

So in His wisdom, God caused Adam to fall into a deep sleep, and from his rib formed the woman, a perfect counterpart for Adam. Adam called her Eve.

God did not create Eve from the dust of the earth as He did Adam because He had already put His characteristics into human form in Adam. To have made a new creation from anything other than what was already in Adam would have been to make something inferior to Adam.

The rib God used to make the woman was symbolic of certain characteristics which God took from Adam to make the woman. The qualities that God placed into Eve are what today we consider to be the woman's nature.

In the nature of God are all the characteristics that are components of mankind. In God are the all-embracing, perfectly balanced characteristics of the disciplinarian and the nurturer, toughness and tenderness, masculinity and femininity.

Marriage, the unifying of husband and wife into "one flesh," represents the bringing together again of these godly characteristics that were invested in man alone, and then separated into male and female.

From man came the woman through creation, and by woman has come man in procreation since then. God's unique balance of life is evident.

Both men and women have part of God's image within them, and both individually glorify God. But, although they each share a common image, they each have a separate human nature.

The man was created from the dust of the earth, and the woman from the rib of the man. That's why it seems natural for a man to be dirty, but it never is for a woman.

However humorous that may sound — think on it.

A man may smoke his cigar, use profanity, and tell his dirty stories, and people accept that as a "man's kind" of way, but it is incongruous to the nature of a woman.

Men and women are unique, and each has their own individual uniqueness.

13

A man was created for the glory of God, and the woman for the glory of the man. But how can a woman be the glory of a man unless that man is becoming the glory of God by being conformed to the image of Christ?

We live in what has been called the "era of the mediocre man," meaning men want authority but not accountability.

Mediocrity is the bane of excellence. Mediocrity begets no glory.

Excellence in spirit begins with having an excellent spirit.

The more Christ-like the man, the greater the glory.

Churchianity and Christianity are not synonymous. Neither are reactions and results. Mediocre men offer God reactions, while God wants results from their lives.

When Jesus Christ healed the blind, He used a different method for every miracle. The touch always produced the same result, but the reactions varied. Today, too many men try to teach the method instead of desiring the touch, and reward reactions instead of results.

The method was instant and the touch was constant.

Transposition is the common error of humanity. Typists transpose letters and write "untie" instead of "unite." Big difference. Transposition will wreak havoc in our lives. Do it with leaded and unleaded gas and it will ruin a car.

You cannot attribute to a work of the flesh what can only be done in the life by the Spirit of God. God's glory in the Old Testament dwelled in the Holy of Holies in an earthly tabernacle made with hands as constructed by Israel. Today — since the advent of Christ — the glory of God resides in tabernacles not made with hands, but in the hearts of men.

"Microwave Christians" want instant salvation, sanctification, and glorification. They don't want to take the time, exercise the patience, determine the will, or pay the

14

price to go through the fire of God's perfecting power that they might be filled with His glory.

Pottery is made strong in a fiery kiln, steel is tempered in a red-hot forge, and men are made when the fire of God burns the dross out of their lives and leaves them filled with the glory of God.

The surgeon doesn't operate on a patient because he delights in pain, but because he loves health and hates disease. So God doesn't do things to our hurt, but to our health.

God does everything for the purpose of revealing more of Himself to us.

Man was created for the glory of God.

The woman was created to be the glory of the man.

A woman glories in her relationship to a man who manifests the nature and image of Christ-likeness.

That's the man God wants you to be.

2
THE UNIQUENESS OF WOMAN

God gave man and woman their own individual, unique nature.

To each of them it is a glory.

The unique desires of each are satisfied differently, the result of God's creative wisdom. The basic differences between the male and the female need to be understood from a Biblical perspective.

Israel's sin was dealing with God as if He were a man. Many a man misses the mark in dealing with a woman because he makes the same mistake: he tries to deal with her as if dealing with a man.

In creation, God put Adam in the Kingdom of God, and the Kingdom of God in Adam, when He placed Adam in Eden and gave him stewardship over the whole earth.

Adam was created in the image of God, and for the glory of God. God created him in a state of concreated holiness, without sin, and therefore with a perfect mind, body and spirit. Thus Adam could exercise obedience to God's command and name everything on earth that needed to be named. Adam's mind was capable of doing it because it was without blight.

Sin brings blight. Adam was without sin, therefore without blight.

To know what Adam was like in his original manhood, you need only to look at the second Adam, the Lord Jesus Christ in His humanity.

Given the responsibility of stewardship over the earth, Adam derived his greatest satisfaction from the reproduction process that God had established for the replenishing of the earth. As steward over the earth, Adam was given the responsibility of overseeing the process of re-creation. His unique nature and desire was basically satisfied in relationship to his stewardship, and the reproductive process involved in it.

From then until now it has never changed. Man still derives his greatest satisfaction from the reproductive process of his stewardship over the earth. His job — whether farming, running a lathe, operating a steel mill, selling clothes, managing a company, digging ditches, or exercising authority as the chief executive officer of a corporation — is still where a man finds his basic satisfaction in life.

The workplace is where a man's unique desire is basically satisfied.

The farmer's satisfaction with the reproductive process is found at harvesttime. A salesman finds it when the customer buys the product or service, an architect when his plans become a finished building, an accountant when his audit is completed, and a preacher when his altar call produces results.

We men were created that way. It's never changed.

God's pattern for the replenishing of the earth through the process of each seed-bearing plant reproducing after its own kind was then transferred to the reproduction process for mankind.

To replenish the earth, God established a reproductive process whereby the man would plant his seed into the woman, and the earth would be replenished with humanity.

Because the reproduction process of replenishing the earth was the most satisfying to a man's unique nature in relationship to his job, it became the same in relationship to a woman. The same principle applied to both stewardships — that of the earth and of the family.

God made sex to be enjoyable so the man would desire it and thus fulfill God's command to replenish the earth. Sex isn't something a man is forced to engage in.

Sex is the most satisfying aspect of a man's life in relationship to a woman.

It is also the reason some men can be satisfied with their paycheck at work and sex at home, and not be too concerned with much of anything else.

Paycheck and sex, and some men are content.

But, that won't satisfy the needs of a woman nor satisfy his God-given responsibilities and character as a man. When a man fails to recognize, understand, or meet the unique needs of a woman, it can cause trouble — for her, for him.

Procreation may be an evidence of manliness, but not of maturity.

There are evidences and provisions of love that every man needs to understand. Love is greater than sex. Sex is not a part of love when it is the expression of lust.

Woman was made to be beautiful, desirable, and loved.

Unfortunately, because of his tendency to worship the creature rather than the Creator, man has often corrupted the natural beauty of woman by looking upon her as simply an object to be taken or bought in order to satisfy his own lust.

Strong words. But true.

It is also true that many a woman thoroughly enjoys her ability to seduce a man, and to exercise power over him through her seductive capabilities. There would be no pornography to look at if there were no women who desired to flaunt their sexual prowess.

The women's liberation movement began as a justifiable rejection against men's double standards, but unfortunately through time it has degenerated into a general rebellion against all men. The rejection of male chauvinism by women was admirable because woman was never meant to be a prey to some man's predatory passions and lusts. Rejection is often a proper course of action, but rebellion never is.

Still, the existence and growth of "women's lib" does serve to illustrate a point. Women are tired of being misunderstood and abused.

Men must learn to minister to the woman's unique nature. Both single and married men need to know and understand the nature of both sexes, but many do not even recognize their own unique male nature. Men complain that they do not understand women, but often they simply do not understand themselves.

To misunderstand women is to misjudge and mistreat them. That's why women suffered from male dominance for centuries.

Christianity is the only religion that has elevated woman to the place God originally created her to be — that of joint-heir with man.

A woman's uniqueness is her greatest appeal to a man — and his greatest challenge.

PART 1:
COMMUNICATION

3

COMMUNICATING WITH GOD

All good communication in life must begin with communication with God. That's where truth is found.

In the parable of "the sower and the seed" our Lord teaches us that immediately after the seed is sown, Satan comes to steal it. The seed is the Word of God, and it is the Word that Satan tries to steal, kill, or destroy.

The devil did it to Adam and Eve. By causing their disobedience to the word, Satan stole the word from them, and brought about cataclysmic change in human society and on earth.

Pharaoh tried to recapture Moses and the children of Israel immediately after they left Egypt. After Elijah's great victory on Mount Carmel, he was immediately threatened by Jezebel, and ran for his life. Herod tried to kill Jesus immediately after His birth, and did destroy all the children in Israel under two years of age.

Immediately after His baptism, Jesus was led into the wilderness and there was tempted of the devil. Satan was trying to steal "the Word." But after overcoming the evil one, Jesus, it is said, "returned in the power of the Spirit."[1]

In the Bible, the number forty designates a probationary period. Forty days the rain was on the earth, forty years the children of Israel wandered in the wilderness, Jesus was in the wilderness being tempted for forty days.

After every great work of God, or a word given from God, there seems to be a probationary period of time during which Satan tries to steal the word or work from the lives of those receiving it. When, as in the case of our Lord, we have overcome the devil during that time of testing, we then return in the power of His Spirit as an "overcomer."

It's the reason why over and over I try to emphasize the truth that the day after the battle is more important than the eve.

Satan's attempts to steal the word are the "Great Rip Off" in men's lives today. Satan not only tries to steal God's Word, but also men's words.

As God's Word is to us, our word is to be to others.

A subtle way to steal a man's word is to tempt him to live in ways that counteract what he says. A man may have a passion for God, yet not love God.

With all due respect to everyone — the truth is that some of the people today telling of their "faith" lead lives that are not compatible with the Word of God, nor consistent with His character.

Jesus said, "He that hath my commandments, and keepeth them, he it is that loveth me."[2] Obedience to the Lord's commandments, His Word, is the evidence of loving Him. Men may have a passion for God, they may need God, know about God, have an experience with God, but still not love God.

Experiencing is no substitute for abiding.

Neither is passion a substitute for love.

Men (or women) who openly tell of, or testify to, their relationship to God must live in obedience to the Word in order to give evidence of their love for God.

Otherwise theirs is a "testi-phony," not a "testimony." Their life is not based on truth.

Satan is a tempter, deceiver, accuser and liar. There is no truth in him.

No lie can serve the purpose of God.

No lie is "white."

The closer a lie is to the truth, the more damning it is.

Unbelief is the basis of sin, pride is the strength of sin, and deceitfulness is the character of sin.

All deceitfulness is a form of lying. Our own heart, in its natural state, is deceptive. It's the reason we must often have an outside, objective opinion as to whether we are right or wrong. The only true way to know right from wrong is to have the Spirit of Truth born into us to witness to the truth of our thoughts, words, motives and deeds.

We don't need Jesus as some form of "fire insurance" to keep us out of hell, but we need His Spirit — which is the Spirit of Truth — to witness constantly to our conscience the truth of our lives. God wants His own to worship Him "in spirit and in truth."[3]

It is in the truth that we share with God, that we build our friendship with God. Prayer is communication with God.

Prayer is not an attempt to convince God of our righteousness, but an opportunity for God to show us His righteousness.

Prayer is not a vain exercise in some religious ritual that acts as a mental purgative, or a spiritual catharsis. Genuine, authentic prayer is dealing with matters of heaven and hell based on the Word of God. It is acknowledging the authority of Christ, submitting to the will of God, taking dominion over matters in the realm of the Spirit, exercising faith in the Word of God, receiving His counsel, subjugating the flesh, subduing Satan, and causing the Kingdom of God to be established on the earth as it is in heaven.

The prayer closet is more important than the Oval Office, has more influence than the United Nations, and can accomplish more than all the dictators in the world

25

combined. Regrettably, many men have been "ripped off" in their prayer life at home, church, and in their community.

Satan laughs at Christians' wishes, but trembles at their intercessions.

How often have I read the letters of men who have written me for counsel, prayer, or help, and have literally wept over their inability to see or understand that their lives are being "ripped off" by the devil. The ability to rise from their pit, escape from their dilemma, to be freed from the shackles that bind them, lies in the truth that Jesus Christ overcame Satan at the cross, and if they go there they will have freedom.

Don't let anyone or anything keep you from your "prayer closet." When you enter, you will find the Lord waiting for you.

Be honest with God.

Don't try to hide anything from Him — from your sins to your feelings.

When you empty yourself, God can fill you with Himself.

After you have talked it all out with God, even if He hasn't yet revealed clearly all the answers you were seeking, you can then go about your regular business and see what He will do.

People and things will let you down.

God never will.

Take it all to Him.

First.

4
YOUR WORD IS YOUR BOND

It was a Thursday night, the first night of a three-day series of meetings that had been planned for months. The pastor was a Barnabas-type man, a good man, full of faith and the Holy Spirit.

Being assured by his people of their support, and with other pastors having assured him of their cooperative support, he had prepared for the meeting by adding extra musicians, chairs and equipment — all at considerable expense.

Almost all of his people indicated, by a show of hands, that they would attend the meetings, even before he had finalized plans for the speaker in what was to be a city-wide event. But throughout the weekend he sat on the platform embarrassed and humiliated when only a small percentage of dedicated people arrived and sat among the roomful of empty chairs.

He offered apologies to the speaker for the poor attendance, assuring his guest that he had done all he could to encourage maximum attendance of all those who had pledged to participate. Then on Sunday the house was full of people who had given their word to attend Thursday, Friday and Saturday, but had not done so. They came to church light-hearted, without a thought in their minds of what they had done to their pastor, the ministry, or to the Lord Himself.

They had given their word, and not kept it.

"Reprove, rebuke, exhort with all longsuffering and doctrine"[1] is what the Apostle Paul wrote to Timothy. They needed that word.

Actually, what those people did was lie to their pastor. They said they would attend and did not do it. They were guilty of worshipping God with their lips, but their heart was not in it.

Because their pastor represents the authority of Christ in the congregation, it was as if they lied to the Lord Himself. The book of Acts records that Ananias and Sapphira lied to the Holy Spirit, and they were both stricken to death for their sin. They were held accountable for their word, which was a lie, in the presence of the entire congregation.

God never gives authority without accountability. But who holds us accountable when we give our word and don't keep it? Many among us have grown up with parents who don't keep their word. Who holds them accountable? Or our boss, friends, neighbors? Who holds *us* accountable for failure to keep *our* word?

As men, we must be mature enough to become accountable for our word — we must see that we keep it when we give it.

One of the reasons many Christians live unfulfilled lives is because they have given God their word, and not kept it. Then they blame God for not answering their prayers or supplying their needs when in fact it is due to their own failure to keep their word.

Many men pile load upon load of guilt upon themselves by not keeping their word, then wonder why they have problems.

A man's name is only as good as his word.

His word is only as good as his character.

True of God — true of men.

A man's word is the expression of his nature.

Scripture says that Jesus Christ came as the "express image" of God.[2] It also records that "in the beginning was the Word, and the Word was with God, and the Word was God."[3] Jesus Christ is the expression of the nature of God.

You can tell a man's character by his words.

God's Word is the sole source of our faith, and the absolute rule of our conduct.

Our word, when given, is a source of faith to those who receive it, and determines their conduct. When a man tells a woman he will take her out for dinner, she acts upon that word and is ready when the time comes. When a supplier tells a contractor he will have the materials at the job site on a certain day, the contractor expects those materials to be there. When the word is not kept, unbelief develops.

The honor of God is the criterion of holiness in relationships.

Being a man of honor is being a man of your word.

Truth is the essence of the word.

Today's society suffers the same ills that plagued Isaiah's day when he declared, "Judgment is turned away backward, and...truth is fallen in the street."[4]

Many men today have little respect for truth. Truth is being literally trampled upon. Authors mix fact and fiction with no apology and call it "faction" or "literary license." Filmmakers do the same and call it "art." Ministers do it and call it "evangelistically speaking." It's a lie by any name.

On a plane recently flying across the country, I saw a film in which a government officer was depicted falsifying a report to the press. A young boy, traveling with his father, was sitting next to me on the plane. Turning to his dad, he asked, "Why did he lie?"

A father who keeps his word can combat the influence of the world on his children and turn to his son and explain the difference between the truth and a lie, along with the consequences of each. But what father can teach his children the importance of keeping their word when he is riddled with guilt for not doing it himself, or when they see the inconsistencies in his own life?

Fathers who punish their children for not keeping their word when they are guilty of the same only teach their children not to get caught.

Our nation has become so cynical toward itself that we do not expect the truth from anyone. Drugs and teenage suicide are epidemic and most of it stems from this very cynicism toward society and self. These are young people who believe in no one, and have hope of nothing.

You can tell the philosophy of a people by the slogans they carry. Today's modern youth carry placards that say, "Self, not society," "Terrorism is a gas," "and "So What?" Life holds no value for them. Abortion means nothing — neither does marriage or money.

Government "disinformation" bureaus have become so effective that the average citizen doesn't know whether what he hears or reads through the media is the truth or just carefully created propaganda.

Not only did Isaiah say that truth was fallen in the street and being trampled upon, but that judgment was turned away backward. Certainly that is the case when the principle of jurisprudence — that a person is presumed innocent until proven guilty — is distorted into the attitude (and often the practice) that a person is labeled guilty until proven innocent.

This situation is particularly disturbing when it is evidenced in the news media. Sometimes members of the press and broadcast industry seem to set themselves up as judge and jury of those they report about. You can see their bias in the adjectives they use, the questions they ask, and the answers they choose to report.

"Victims have rights too," proclaims a sign on the wall of a Southern California courtroom. How sad that we have to remind ourselves of that fact.

It is further evidence that we live in a perverted world.

On the day of Pentecost, Peter gave a charge to his hearers that is still good today when he preached, "Save yourselves from this untoward generation."[5]

Some of the same people who argue for the abolishment of the death penalty contend for abortion. That's perversion.

God calls His people a "peculiar people."[6] It is not because of their style of dress, methods of worship, manners, or idioms of speech, but because they love. And, they love truth.

The evidence of a changed life in conversion is first a love for God, second a love for the Word, and third a love of the brethren.

Sometimes it seems that men who love truth are an anomaly in today's society, an anachronistic and archaic throwback to another age. Often they are viewed with contempt by colleagues because of their refusal to compromise truth or principle. Many times bosses are hesitant to hire people of real integrity because they are afraid they might expose the unethical behavior and fradulent practices prevalent in the workplace. Honest scholars have been turned out of their academic programs because they refused to manipulate or fabricate data.

The only place men who love truth are popular is in heaven — or among other men of "goodwill."

Roy brought his son-in-law to our "52 Hours of Courage" meeting in Newport Beach because he thought being with other godly men would do him some good. The son-in-law had just been fired from his position as a regional sales manager because he would not fabricate reports or expense accounts. Standing for right cost him his job, but it made him more of a man.

The contest between truth and a lie is constant. To be able to walk in truth, every man needs to be grounded in the Word of Truth, and submitted to the Spirit of Truth which bears witness with his own spirit.

No lie can serve the purposes of God.

Knowing the truth and not living it is a lie in itself.

Knowing you gave your word and did not keep it is living a lie.

Knowing you gave your word but need to rescind it, or repent of it, and not doing it is living a lie.

When you have spoken a hasty word, the best thing to do is to go ask forgiveness and try to get out of that negative situation. This is true even if the word is to a five-year-old daughter who cannot possibly understand why a business trip is pushing her weekend with Daddy back by seven days.

Small children do not know the difference between a broken promise and a lie.

As a man, you must have integrity before God and man — and even before children, especially your own!

God says we are going to give an account of every "idle word."[7] Telling someone you will do something simply to pacify them, without meaning to do what you promise, is an "idle word." God holds us accountable for such words even though men may not. Such words are often the cause of mediocrity, lost opportunities, lack of favor, and burdened minds.

"The curse causeless shall not come,"[8] is what God's Word says.

There is a cause for every curse.

Some men need to think back, find what idle words they have spoken, what vows they have made to God and broken, what promises to their families they have not kept, and repent of it so they can be rid of the results of walking "after the flesh," and not "after the Spirit."[9]

Larry is a friend of mine who was entering a new phase of life, joining a new company, and engaging a new partner. However, he lacked peace concerning what he was doing. He was troubled.

Peace is the umpire for doing the will of God.

Many's the man who missed God's way because he based his decision on outward circumstances rather than an inward witness.

God was faithful to Larry, and from the morning devotional reading of Proverbs came a word leaping out of the pages at him.

"Son, if you endorse a note for someone you hardly know, guaranteeing his debt, you are in serious trouble. You may have trapped yourself by your agreement. Quick! Get out of it if you possibly can! Swallow your pride; don't let embarrassment stand in the way. Go and beg to have your name erased. Don't put it off. Do it now. Don't rest until you do. If you can get out of this trap you have saved yourself like a deer that escapes from a hunter, or a bird from the net."[10]

The truth was so real and powerful to Larry that it almost took his breath away. He knew it was true, and he knew he was going through with the arrangement with the new partner only because he had given his word and did not want to back out of it. Though he knew he should back out of the agreement, his pride would not let him do it. When he heard God's Word say, "Swallow your pride," it hit him like a ton of bricks, and he knew what he had to do.

It wasn't easy. It took some long, hard discussions, but he was able to get out of his agreement without any loss.

Pride is the strength of sin.

Pride won't let us humble ourselves to admit wrong, or even suffer being wronged.

When the Bible speaks of the man "that sweareth to his own hurt, and changeth not"[11] it does not mean to imply that a man shouldn't repent if he has done wrong. It simply means that in the integrity of a man's character he will keep his word. Period.

Jephthah, in the Bible, lost his daughter as a result of a hasty word. Because he would not admit he was wrong, he was responsible for the loss of his daughter's life.

"Death and life are in the power of the tongue,"[12] says Proverbs.

Satan not only wants to "rip off" God's Word from men's lives, he also wants to steal their word. If the devil can cause a man to fail to keep his word, he can keep that man from total manhood.

Richard dropped out of church. He had made a promise to contribute to the building fund of his church, developed financial problems, could not keep his promise, and rather than go face the pastor and tell him what had happened, he simply stopped going to church. It affected his entire life and family. He lost out because he didn't deal with realities through truth and godly character.

What Richard needed to know was that the enemy of his soul, Satan himself, probably caused his misfortune to prohibit the payment of his promised contribution. "Divide and conquer" is not a divine principle, but a devilish one.

No matter what others do, keep your heart and mind clear and clean by washing them constantly with the water of the Word of God. Then your words will follow with truth and integrity.

Great works are built on great words.

Let your words be great in God.

Let God be great in your words.

Be a man of *the* Word, and a man of *your* word.

5

A COVENANT WORD
IN MARRIAGE

My daughter was engaged to a man and their wedding was only weeks away. He had proposed, she had accepted, and from then on our house was a constant bedlam of planning, phoning, preparing and partying.

Flowers were bought, the church rented, invitations printed, and bridesmaids' dresses ordered. Then, six weeks before the wedding, the groom called wanting to postpone the ceremony. My daughter was depressed, my wife distraught, and they asked me what to do.

"Cancel the wedding," I said. "If your fiance's word is no better than what he has indicated thus far, then you have no business marrying him."

They agreed. The wedding was canceled.

My daughter went on to law school and while there met a man with whom she fell in love. She graduated, married, passed her bar exams, and today is happily married with two children, and works as a Deputy District Attorney in California.

The decision to cancel the wedding was a tough one to make, and the days after it were not easy, but it was the right thing to do. Although it was my daughter's life, I was accountable to God for the stewardship of my family. Being a good steward meant exercising authority when it was needed. My daughter and her husband thank me today for helping her make a decision that was too difficult for her to make on her own.

How can a woman trust a man if she can't trust his word?

The ability to trust her husband's word is the ability to trust her husband. *Trust is extended to the limit of a man's word and no more.*

Trust makes vulnerability possible. Lack of trust makes it impossible.

The vows of marriage are not merely a sexual agreement that remain unbroken except by adultery.

The vows of marriage, whichever ones are recited, are a holy commitment before God in which a man accepts the responsibility of his manhood in relation to his wife. God views those vows as evidence of the man's desire to love his wife just as Christ loves the Church. When a man breaks the law of love, he has broken his vows and weakened his covenant with his wife.

Every principle in human life emanates from, is originated in, or is initiated by the Kingdom of God.

The evidence and provisions of love are those in God's own nature that we find manifest or required in our lives. When God tells us in His Word that as men we are to love our wives as Christ loves the Church, it behooves us to know HOW Christ loves the Church so we can know how to love our wives.

The evidences of love are selflessness, the desire to benefit the one loved, and a desire for unity.

We know God as the one true God monotheistically; but we experience His love and grace in our lives polytheistically. God is God, but manifest as Father, Son and Holy Spirit. The Apostle John wrote about it best when he stated that God loves us so much that He willingly gave His only begotten Son to pay the price for our salvation, and then sent His Spirit to produce eternal life in us who believe on His Son.

God's selflessness is seen in the Father's willingness to give His Son *in place of* us, Christ the Son's willingness to give Himself *for* us, and the Holy Spirit's willingness to be given *to* us.

God's desire for our benefit is best stated by the psalmist when he wrote of the Lord: ''...no good thing will he withhold from them that walk uprightly.''[1] Scripture states emphatically that if God loved us enough to send Christ to die for us when we were still at enmity with Him because of our sin, how much more will He freely give us all things now that we are part of His family through the New Birth.

How can we not understand God's desire for our unity with Him when Christ Himself prayed in His great high-priestly prayer that we might ''be one'' with each other and with the Father, even as He was one with God.[2] God's whole purpose in redemption is to bring us into a place of ultimate intimacy with Him as ''sons of God.''[3]

These evidences of love in the very nature of God are then evidences of love in our lives as well. We see evidence of this love when men risk their lives in an attempt to rescue a loved one in danger. We also see evidence of this love in the daily routine of rising to go to work, when the body and soul would rather rest, all for the sake of those loved ones who are dependent upon that self-sacrifice.

Such selflessness can be both exotic and mundane, but it does reveal the nature of love in the human creature.

Love focuses on the one loved, with thought of self secondary. Lust, which is perverted love, focuses on self at the expense of the other person.

The provisions of love are identity, security and stability.

These are what Christ provides for the Church and what men are to provide their wives and families.

When a woman takes a man's name in marriage, it is her visible expression of submission in relationship which means that if the woman is willing to assume the man's name, then his responsibility is to give her an identity in his character and worth that she can be pleased to identify with.

If your wife is willing to bear your name and children, then you must be willing to bear the responsibility of providing for her and them an identification that is valuable to the worth of their own beings.

A woman's security is not primarily found in her home, but in her relationship to her husband. Infidelity, or a break of marriage vows, shakes and destroys that security. Once shaken, it is difficult to replace without the grace of God in the life.

Because men have been untrustworthy, many women are rebelling against taking the man's name in marriage, or depending upon the husband for any security. The reason many women today are working is not simply because they want to have a career of their own, or the help of a second income, but because they desire security if or when their husband leaves.

Pre-nuptial contracts, which are so prevalent today, are attempts to find security in and from a relationship. What a sad commentary on the status of manhood that women today feel they must seek a legal guarantee of security and provision because they are unable to depend on the moral responsibility of their mates.

Even the man who is content with renting all his life and never seeks to own a home of his own, often does not realize that some of the source of distress, discontentment and disagreement in his family comes from his wife's inability to have a place to call her own. A woman has a "nesting instinct," particularly when having children, that is fulfilled when she can paint, paper, decorate and renovate to satisfy her need for security. Instead of providing a sense of stability, the lifestyle of the typical male often produces a sense of instability.

The instability affects his children as well.

Stability in the man's character translates to normality in his children.

The way the Bible states it is, "Reverence for God gives a man deep strength; his children have a place of refuge and security."[4] Children's security comes from the father's inner stability in his relationship with God.

Giving your word in marriage: It is not something to be done frivolously.

Words can unite or separate, bless or curse, heal or wound, edify or demolish, create or destroy, enlighten or obscure, liberate or enslave.

As long as a man's words live, he lives; when his words cease, he ceases. Great men are known by the greatness of their words.

Words live or die, grow or wither. Lincoln's Gettysburg address contains only a few words, but those words have grown in importance and significance over the years. Yet when originally spoken, those simple words were regarded almost with disdain, while the grandiose words of the eloquent Mr. Douglas, Lincoln's counterpart, were greatly admired — for a brief time. Today the words of Lincoln are revered, while those of his contemporary are lost in oblivion.

Jesus Christ said, "The words that I speak unto you, they are spirit, and they are life."[5]

His words, when sown in the heart of a man by the Spirit of God, produce life. They are an incorruptible seed, bearing the fruit of eternal life in those who receive them.

A man's words are sown into the lives of those around him and bear the fruit of the type of seed contained in the words. His further action based upon his own words sows for more fruit. If he sows good words, and then acts to keep his word, he will experience a harvest of good fruit in his family.

The word a man keeps begins at the place of commitment in marriage. If his character is not good before marriage, he will have a difficult time trying to produce a good character and keep his word after marriage, regardless of how strong the feelings of love are within him. Love must be disciplined to be fruitful.

Tony attended the church that I pastored. He was large of body, small of spirit, and the biggest thing about him was his mouth. One day in a rare moment of reality when he was seeking a change in his life, he confessed to me what a habitual liar he was.

"My lying is so bad that at times I have to take a little notebook with me to write down what I tell people so I will know what was said the next time I meet them," he admitted.

What a heavy burden to bear. He could have been rid of that yoke if he had been honest with God and truly repented of his sin. Christ's yoke of truth would have freed him from his burden.

His wife knew he loved her, but he could never follow through on that love with corresponding words and actions, and eventually such a wall of mistrust was built up that she divorced him.

Love and trust go hand in hand.

We love God because we know we can trust Him. We trust Him because He loves us.

God is true to His Word in His love for us. We experience it in His selflessness, desire to benefit us, and desire for unity.

God's love for us provides us with a sense of identity, security, and stability.

The man who is considering marriage would do well to count the costs of the word he gives in marriage. The Bible teaches us to count the cost, and not to begin work until we are sure we can afford to. Men must be prepared to open themselves to the Lord for Him to work in their hearts enabling them to love as He loves. Men must prepare their character to give integrity to the name they expect their wives to identify with.

Loving a woman as Christ loves the Church takes time, humility, patience on both parts — the husband's and the wife's — and it also takes a lot of time in prayer.

The rewards, however, for accepting the responsibility God has given us as men, are plentiful. The rewards of a peaceful heart, a good marriage, a fulfilled wife and happy children are worth more than all the money you will ever earn in your life. The disciple John wrote, "I have no greater joy than to hear that my children walk in truth."[6]

Embracing truth, keeping it in your life through your word and your fulfillment of God's plan of action for your life, will allow you to lead your family in truth, and give you your greatest satisfaction in your old age.

A man of God:

1 — Loves the woman God gives him as Christ loved the Church.

2 — Leads his family in truth by keeping his word.

3 — Gives his word in marriage and keeps it, however difficult it is at times.

A woman and family can live on that man's word forever.

They can depend on him.
So can the world.
So can God.

6
WORD, GESTURE, AND SPIRIT

We were standing on a riverbank on the backside of a resort in the middle of Alaska. The river's rushing, hissing sound, and the gurgling of the little pools that formed along its banks, were a background to the young man's voice as he poured out to me his innermost concern and need.

"She left me," he was saying about his wife. "I came home one day and she was gone. I knew we were having some problems, but I never thought they were that serious."

The young man had married the day after graduation from Bible college. Two weeks later the couple had left for Alaska where he had hoped to assist a church and its pastor. There was little pay, a stark house away from town, few friends, and little companionship for the young bride since her new husband was gone much of the time trying to establish himself both in the ministry and on the job. It was a struggle all the way.

After he had finished telling me how things had been for the past year and a half, I reached up, placed my arms around his neck, and very softly and gently told him, face to face, the hard truth.

"You are dumb," I said.

His eyes widened with astonishment. He was looking for pity, sympathy, comfort, and I was giving him truth.

"Moses' zeal for God caused him to commit murder, and because of it he had to spend forty years on the backside of the desert," I told him. "Your zeal has almost caused you to kill a marriage."

"What do you mean?" he asked, moving away from me to sit down.

"I'll explain it to you," I said, and began to point out his error and what he could do about it.

His zeal for what he desired in life had blinded him to the needs of his wife. There was a reason God provided for newly married men in Israel to be exempt for an entire year from army duty which would necessitate absence from their wives. God knew they needed time to develop a relationship in marriage before any separation or stress could be placed on that fresh and fragile union.

Without thought to his wife's needs, this young man had been content to satisfy himself at her expense. He had found Alaska exhilarating, and the lack of funds no obstacle to his personal fulfillment as a ministerial assistant.

Obviously his wife had felt differently. Every woman needs love's provisions of identity, security and stability. He had been too wrapped up in his own ambitions to provide even one of these. He had taken his bride directly from a stable environment at home and had thrust her into a new and different situation which robbed her of all the stabilizing influences in her life. Then there had come a burden of financial stress she had never known before. She had not found "living by faith" for each meal to be an exciting time of spiritual enrichment as he did. The pressure of a congregation that expected her to be something she wasn't, and to know already things she didn't know, was hurtful to her. No matter how hard she tried, she felt she wasn't good enough to satisfy her husband and the congregation.

The cold indifference of the senior pastor to their plight, and her first experience with the attitude that they were expected to "pay their dues" to become ministers was far from the experience she had had with her own pastor and their church friends. Altogether, these pressures and incongruities had made an intolerable situation, one for which she was not equipped to cope.

Her love for her husband, her womanliness that desired to see her man succeed, her Christian principles that caused her to feel that to complain would be sin, these had made her cautious in her remarks to her husband. And he, absorbed in his own interests, had missed entirely the subtle but persistent indications of her deep-seated unhappiness.

His religious upbringing had taught him to equate prayer with an altar in a church ceremony, so there had not even been a time of prayer in the home during which she could have let out the pain she was suffering. This is one of the reasons why shared prayer is crucial to a marriage. If this couple had prayed together, they would likely have had better communication with each other, and could have avoided the ruptured relationship with its hurt and grief.

The young husband loved his wife. What he lacked was the knowledge of what is needed to make a good marital union. He was putting ministry ahead of marriage.

His wife knew he loved her, and she loved him, but she was not able to get through to him, and finally she had had enough. She called her parents, they sent money, and she flew off to Mom, Dad, home and security. She left her husband a note telling him not to follow her.

His sorrow after her leaving had been compounded by her note of rejection. It had created in him a sense of despair, a feeling of "what's the use?" His negative, hopeless attitude had sparked in him the thought of running away up to the Prudhoe Project, which was even farther north, where he could stay hidden away from everyone for a couple of years.

The young man had failed. God's Word says that we are to be swift to hear and slow to speak; but he had transposed those phrases and had become swift to speak and slow to hear. As a result, he had not only perverted the principle, he had also jeopardized his marriage. Now he wanted desperately for me to tell him what to do.

He explained that he had already inquired and found a position near her parents' hometown where he could be an assistant pastor, but that he was still considering just giving up and going north.

Rejection is the hardest thing for a man to take. Fear of rejection the second time was a barrier to this young man's pursuit of a wife he loved very much, the wife God had made him a steward of.

"Son, don't add stupidity to dumbness," I said.

Then I explained to him that the job as an assistant pastor might be God's opportunity for him to be placed right where his wife was. God was giving him a second chance to ask forgiveness and win her back. It might take a second courtship, starting at square one and doing it all over again, but it would be infinitely worth the effort to regain what he had lost in his ignorance.

"Don't let your natural male ego and pride keep you from humbling yourself and allowing God to put your marriage, ministry and life back together again," I told him.

"Do you really think the Lord would do that?" he asked.

"Jesus Christ is your Savior," I said. "He didn't promise just to save your soul. He is your Savior maritally, emotionally, financially, socially and every other way. He is the Great Physician Who can heal every hurt. If you don't know that, and experience His healing in your own life, how can you minister to others effectively?"

This man wanted an escape, but he was trying to escape *from* the bad situation, instead of *to* a better one. He did not understand that God didn't just deliver us *from* sin, but *to* righteousness. To deliver us *to* righteousness, He must first deliver us *from* sin.

When God makes a way of escape, it is not *from*, but *to*. God was making a way for him to escape *to* his wife, not *from* her. Man's way is to escape *from* everything, regardless of where he is escaping to. God's way is to escape to reconciliation, a resurrected marriage, and a better life than man has ever known before.

"Don't blow it again," I said to him. "Go!"

This young man not only needed to learn what his responsibilities and priorities were in relationship to God and his wife, he also needed to learn the three elements of communication that would enable him to have a successful marriage.

The three methods of communication given to men are word, gesture, and spirit. We often communicate with our words, but our gestures and spirits confirm or deny those words. Thus, the old axiom, "Actions speak louder than words."

For the young minister, the method of communication he needed to employ was gesture — he needed to go to his wife.

Second, he needed to communicate in spirit — he needed to let her know by his attitude that he cared about her feelings.

Third, he needed to communicate in words — he needed to tell her that he loved her and wanted to make things right in their marriage.

Communication by spirit is so important. The newlywed I was talking to could have achieved so much in his marriage and have avoided so much pain, if he had understood how prayer together would help him and his wife to unite in spirit and communicate on that deepest level.

Too many times the lack of communication in spirit which comes from not praying together produces an inability to verbalize inmost feelings.

Communication by gesture is the second most important method of communication. Gesture confirms the word, the spirit seals it.

Words are sometimes the most visible evidence of what is in a man's heart, and a way we are able to see his character even without being close to him. But when a man is within the context of a family situation, the other members are able to see just as visibly his communication of gesture and spirit. He must send the same message all three ways.

Any communication implies both a sender and a receiver. For perfect communication, the receiver must receive exactly what was sent. Any imperfection of that message is a distortion.

Distortion is the variable sound of the radio signals when they are not strong enough, or when there is interference. Distortion is the television picture filled with snow, wiggling lines, or blurred pictures.

Distortion also occurs when the person hearing misunderstands what was said, or repeats it differently from the way it was first uttered. Some people, like the communists, deliberately distort communications. Distortion prevents good communication.

''Reliable communication permits progress,''[1] is the proverb.

The sender and receiver must be on the same wave length for good communication, whether in radio, television, or person to person.

When husband and wife disagree, it is easy for them to distort meanings, to twist them to their own ends, or to pervert them to prevent reconciliation.

When communication stops, abnormality sets in, and the ultimate end of abnormality is death. This occurs when a leaf is severed from the stem and then withers and dies.

Marriages die when the married couple refuses to communicate or when too much distortion prevents understanding and reconciliation.

Faith dies when men refuse to communicate with God or when His words become distorted to them. God says what He means, and means what He says. It is necessary to be born again of His Spirit to understand His Word properly. People who have never received the Spirit of Christ into their lives cannot understand the Bible as those who have received that Spirit.

Sin always causes distortion.

Men must keep their minds clear and their hearts clean in order to prevent as much distortion as possible in their lives. The more righteous the person, the less distortion in his life, and the more clearly he can communicate and receive communications, both with God and man.

Swift to hear and slow to speak, that is the rule for communication that desires to exhibit love. It is the way God communicates with us. It is the way He wants us to learn to communicate with those we love as well.

Communication.

For a husband, communication includes listening to his wife, and thereby ministering to her need for someone who will listen, who will care about the details of her life.

The man who understands and values communication will listen to his children, even the babbling of a six-year-old, or the bad news from a sixteen-year-old.

The man who communicates will openly confess his love with words and confirm it with gesture and in spirit.

There is a three-word formula for success in real estate. It is, ''Location, location, location.''

There is a three-word formula for success in a man's life. It is, "Communication, communication, communication."

7

TAKING ACTION

Robert had been married for almost thirty years. He had four boys and a thriving business. Unfortunately, however, his marriage was dull and lifeless. There seemed to be no real shared intimacy or communication between him and his wife. Part of the problem was his inability to express his feelings in words.

Attending one of our meetings for men only, he heard something he had never heard before about communication. Meditating on it for weeks, he finally decided to take action.

He began his communication with his wife on that first, fateful day by leaving her a little inexpensive gift on the dresser in the bedroom. His heart was in his throat as he left for work. Fear of rejection, feeling silly after all these years, excited at his timid approach to tell his wife how he felt, all these emotions coursed through him.

When he got home that evening, his wife never mentioned the gift, and neither did he.

The next day, he left something for her in the kitchen. She never mentioned it that evening either, and neither did he.

Every day after that, he continued to leave something for her somewhere in the house where she could find it during the course of her day. They never spoke to one another about it. He would just leave the little gift each day and she would find it.

After about two weeks of this routine, Robert's wife found herself unable to start her day until she had searched the house for whatever her husband had left that morning. The little "treasure hunt" became her daily stimulant. In spite of her age, maturity, and the wisdom of her years, she could not help but delight in the little signs of affection her husband was displaying.

A month later Robert came home one day to find his middle-aged wife wearing a new dress and sporting a new, fashionable hairstyle. Another month went by and he noticed that she had lost some of the bulge that had built up over the years. Before his eyes, his wife began to take on the attitude and appearance of the beautiful young woman he had first become infatuated with, and he fell completely in love with her again.

Four months later they were at a resort, taking what they called a "thirty-year-delayed honeymoon."

To this day neither one of them has ever mentioned the gifts which Robert still leaves daily for her. He found it hard to say what he felt, but he learned he could show it through a "daily dose" of loving communication by gesture.

Robert and his wife had not had a terrible marriage or a failing business. They were normal, Christian people going about their daily, dull routine. But by one small act of personal communication, their whole lives were changed.

Robert didn't use material things as a substitute for his attention and affection, but he used them properly as an expression of his attention and affection.

Gestures communicate.

One evening a woman stopped me as I was entering a church to minister. She asked me please to tell the men in the conference to send their wives birthday and anniversary cards. I smiled and replied that my name wasn't Hallmark, but that I would mention it. She persisted, saying that words simply were not enough, that her husband's actions would communicate so much better that he appreciated her.

Words alone don't satisfy — actions do.

Isn't that what Jesus Christ said to us? "Not every one that saith unto me, Lord, Lord, shall enter into the kingdom of heaven; but he that doeth the will of my Father which is in heaven."[1] The Apostle James echoed this same truth when he wrote, "Faith without works is dead."[2]

How can a man say he loves God, and truly mean it, without proving it by his actions? The same is true of his love for his wife, family and friends.

Gestures can bless or curse, just as our words can. The hand that caresses is the same hand that spanks.

Sailors using semaphore communicate by gesture. Lovers speak volumes with just a slight touch, a light squeeze of the hand, or a meeting of the eyes across a crowded room. Some parents can control their children by the slightest arch of the eyebrow which the child has learned to understand. Referees and umpires use standardized gestures to indicate calls, while coaches talk to players from the sidelines in coded hand signals. Husbands say it with flowers. Governments watch to see who "blinked." Businessmen test the firmness of the handshake. They all communicate by gesture.

The greatest gesture of love known to mankind was the cross of Calvary. Jesus was God's ultimate gesture of love to us. "For God so loved . . . he gave his only begotten Son."[3]

The gesture gives meaning to the words.

Think of the couple who come home in the evening after they have both worked a full day. While he takes the newspaper into the living room and makes himself comfortable in front of the television set, she begins to fix dinner. After dinner he returns to his easy chair while she cleans the table, the dishes, the kitchen, and the children.

Busily she takes the dirty laundry to the washer, loads what she washed that morning into the dryer, then feeds the fish, the dog, and the cat while the children take their baths. She gets them out of the tub and into pajamas, then sits at the table to oversee homework.

Later, after everything is finally done for the evening, she settles wearily into a chair next to her husband and heaves a sigh of relief. Lazily, he opens his eyes, smiles, and reaches for her hand to give it a squeeze. She knows what he is thinking.

"Do you love me?" she asks.

"You know I do, Sweetheart," he responds.

"Really, do you?" she insists.

"I really, really do," he assures her.

"Then prove it."

Gesture is the confirmation of the word. This woman wants some gesture of love from her husband, not just sweet talk.

Many men do not realize that a vacuumed rug or a washed dish during the day can produce wonders in the relationship, especially in the bedroom at night.

For almost as many years as Nancy and I have been married, I have always done the dishes after we have entertained company. If Nancy is loving, gracious, and kind enough to take the time and make the effort to cook and serve, the least I can do is to wash the dishes (and pots, pans, and kitchen floor, as well).

Gestures count.

A young lady in Dallas, Texas, came to me after being in one of our services. Her story is tragic, but one that is repeated countless thousands of times in young girls' lives every day.

"Dr. Cole," she said, "last night in your meeting I forgave my father. I didn't have to forgive him for abusing me, or for anything he did to me. I had to forgive him what he *didn't* do.

"All my life as I was growing up, he never showed me any sign of affection. Because of that neglect, and because I wanted so desperately to feel the affection of a man, I sought attention any way I could and became promiscuous. It almost completely ruined my life. Only Jesus saved me from a fate worse than death. But I just wanted to tell you so that when you talk to men you can tell them how important it is for fathers to show their love."

This young woman had suffered actual emotional deprivation while growing up in a normal, middle-class, Christian home.

Everyone needs to be fed emotionally, as well as physically.

When God created the woman, he designed her physically to be able to breastfeed while cradling her baby in her arms. As the infant nurses at the mother's breast, it is fed physically and emotionally while gazing up into the loving eyes of its mother.

Bottle-fed babies who are given nourishment in a crib and seldom know the embrace of a nursing mother can become emotionally deprived in infancy, and the results can cause problems later on in life. "Love-starved" is not just a colloquial expression.

It is imperative that men learn to show their affection by gesture, regardless of how difficult it may be for them.

Many men are unable to love or be loved normally because of the lack of affection and attention in their own childhood.

In Toronto, when I mentioned this fact in a meeting, I was amazed at the number of men who seem to fall into this category. There were approximately a thousand men in attendance, and when I called for those who wanted me to let them experience for the first time a "father's hug," an avalanche of over three hundred men jammed the aisles.

Later, in Tulsa, a young professor of English at one of the major universities spoke up and told me (in front of the entire audience of men) that he had come to that meeting for the express purpose of getting a "father's hug."

It was in that same city that I made the mistake of asking a group of women how many had never received a father's hug. In response to my offer to supply that gesture for them, over four hundred and fifty out of the thousand ladies in attendance lined up.

I'll never forget that night because when it was all over I had powder, lipstick, mascara, and rouge all over my shirt and coat!

But such incidents were valuable lessons to me concerning what is happening in our homes today. They also made me aware of one of the major causes of divorce in our society — men who do not know how to communicate love. They may say it, but they don't show it.

A man must support his words with his actions. He not only needs to keep his word, he also needs to confirm it with a gesture — a touch, card, gift, phone call, thank-you note, whatever.

The Bible records that there were ten lepers healed by Jesus, but only one turned to give thanks. This man confirmed the work of God in his life with a gesture of gratitude.

Gratitude is the essence of praise, and praise is the essence of worship.

Show your wife and children your love by giving them a gesture of love today.

Show your dad you have become a man by giving him a hug. So what if he has never hugged you in your life? You're a man now — you do the manly thing.

Robert, whom I mentioned earlier, felt like he had found the "fountain of youth" when he learned to communicate by gesture. But don't wait thirty years to get started.

Today is the only day you have. Yesterday is gone, tomorrow is not here. All you have is today. Do it now.

8
SPIRIT TO SPIRIT

"May I sit down?" he asked as he took a seat.

I had thought to say, "No," but it was too late.

The morning sessions of the conference in Pennsylvania where I was speaking were over, and I was ready to enjoy a moment's respite by myself during the lunch hour, before returning to my room to pack. Courtesy dictated that I listen. I'm glad I did.

He said God had changed his life as a result of our ministry.

He had attended a meeting in which I had spoken; he had read one of our books, soberly weighed what was said and then endeavored to put some of the principles of the Bible into practice in his life.

The principle that prayer produces intimacy had really impressed him, and he desired to put that into practice in his marriage. Also, the recommendation that men read from the book of Proverbs in the morning, and from Psalms at night seemed right to him.

However, at night there never seemed to be a time or place for Psalms and prayer. Finally he and his wife agreed that after the children had gone to bed in the evening, before doing anything else, they would read a Psalm and pray together. Not wanting to disturb the children, the couple decided it would be best for them to read and pray in their bedroom.

During their seven years of marriage, they had had continuous problems concerning their sex life. But after three months of reading the Word of God and praying together, they noticed that without even realizing what was happening, their problems had been resolved.

He was so sincere as he said, "When you said prayer produces intimacy, you weren't kidding."

As they prayed together, they began to communicate spirit to spirit. They discovered a new ability to talk about things they had never been able to discuss before. The result of both was intimacy in marriage.

He was elated with his discovery not only of the intimacy of prayer, but also of the intimacy in marriage that prayer and personal communication bring.

Communicating spirit to spirit is the most intimate form of communication possible.

Gerald lives in San Jose, California, and wrote to tell me something in his life so remarkable he could not keep it to himself. He said it was like the experience Peter had when the Lord asked him three times, "Lovest thou me?"[1]

Gerald told me that while seeking God in earnest prayer concerning his marriage he heard the voice of the Lord ask him, "Why do you want your marriage to be O.K.?"

In the privacy of his prayer closet, Gerald answered the Lord honestly, "To get my wife off my back!"

A second time there came the same question from the Lord, "Why do you want your marriage to be O.K.?"

Giving it a second thought, Gerald replied, "So I can live in peace."

For the third time God's voice asked him, "Why do you want your marriage to be O.K.?"

This time Gerald responded with a question of his own, "Lord, why *do* I want my marriage to be O.K.?"

"To glorify Me," was the word he received.

"When I heard that," Gerald wrote, "I got myself right with God first, then started to make the marriage right. I just want to tell you it is getting better and better every day. I never knew a man could love a woman the way I love my wife."

To glorify God is to reveal or manifest His Presence in and through our lives. Jesus said, "Herein is my Father glorified."[2] By His words and actions, Jesus was able to reveal and manifest the Presence of the Father on the earth.

That's God's desire for us.

Every word we speak releases the spirit in which it is spoken.

There is a witness, or a communication in the spirit, that is clearly known and understood. How many times have you heard someone say something and somehow knew that what they were saying was not true? Your spirit witnessed to you about their dishonesty.

Forgiveness is never only in word, but always in spirit. Forgiveness can never be earned, it is always a gift. Always a gift by grace.

Ted obviously did not understand about communication in spirit, or he would never have called me as he did. I was sitting in my office which was located near the beach. (This was several years ago — how I wish I still had that office!) The sliding glass door was open, and I was just relaxing for a moment or two, when the phone rang. It was Ted.

"I've got a problem, and there is really no one else I can talk to," he began. No salutation, no greeting, although we had not seen each other for several years after having worked closely together in a ministry on the East Coast.

"Hi, Ted," I answered. "Go ahead."

"Oh . . . Hi, Ed . . . listen, this thing is really bugging me. I don't know what to do about it. In the last few weeks, my thought life has been horrible. I have some morally impure thoughts — you know, dirty ones — and I've never had them before in my life. My wife and I get along great, no problem there. I'm happy in my work at the radio station. But suddenly, about a month ago, this thing started with my mind, and I don't know what to do about it. I need your help. It's driving me crazy!"

We talked for the next half-hour or so, trying to get at what might be the cause for the sudden barrage of impure thoughts that were obviously putting Ted into a panic. We discussed everything about his wife, former relationships, and went on through the list.

"Tell me about the people you work with. What are they like?" I finally asked him.

He proceeded to tell me about each of his co-workers, describing the secretaries, receptionist, and salesmen who worked with him. From his descriptions, everyone sounded like solid, normal people without serious problems. But I asked him to tell me again about the receptionist.

"Nothing wrong with her," he began. "She's a preacher's wife, probably reaching forty. Seems like a nice lady. Come to think of it, though, there has been a change in her lately."

"What kind of change?" I asked.

"In fact, I can see her now through the window of my office," he said. "She's sitting at her desk doing some work . . . but you know, she's dressing differently these days from when she first came to work here."

"How's that?" I asked.

"She's dressing in tighter-fitting clothes. More provocative. And, come to think of it, a week ago while she was on her coffee break I discovered her reading some magazines that I didn't think a minister's wife would read

— kind of free and sexy. Yeah . . . she's been acting like this for weeks.''

''What is her husband like?'' I asked, and then started to answer my own question. ''Straight-laced, legalistic, religious, meticulous, detail-oriented and somewhat cold in personality?''

''Yeah, I'd say he is,'' Ted responded. ''But how did you know?''

''Ted, let me tell you what could have happened,'' I answered. ''It sounds like that preacher's wife may have reached a point in her life that she has begun to desire some things that she has never desired before. She probably wants some spice in her life, but her husband is just giving her salt.''

Ted was plainly curious about what I was saying, but was astonished that I would venture to make remarks about the sex lives of people I didn't even know.

''Look, Ted,'' I explained, ''just because a person is a Christian doesn't mean he understands how to enjoy God's creation, and sex is a part of it. It is very typical for some religious people to think that sex is something only for those who are carnal-minded. This lady's husband could well be one of those who think that way. For all you know, he might believe it is a sin for him and his wife to want each other physically. His wife could be simply reacting to his restrictive attitude by seeking some personal liberty. When people begin to react in that way, it is often at the expense of their relationship with God, but it's not altogether an uncommon thing.''

''And so you are saying that I'm picking up on her frustration, or thought waves, and am being affected by what is in her spirit?'' Ted asked.

''You're in broadcasting, Ted,'' I said. ''You tell me.''

Ted didn't seem to understand at first that we all communicate, or broadcast for that matter, whatever is in our spirit. In his conscious mind he hadn't even noticed the woman he had described to me. But her spirit had got through to his spirit. When he thought about it consciously, he could remember those signals she had been sending for weeks. They were there, he simply wasn't aware of them until we spoke that day.

"Ed, what will I do?" he asked. "What *can* I do?"

I gave him the four options I could see in that situation and astonished him even further.

"One, if it's true, you can try to minister to her and win her back to a state of real unity with the Lord and with her husband.

"Two, you can resign your job and go somewhere else.

"Three, you can fire her.

"Four, you can have sex with her."

"What! I don't want to do *that*!" was Ted's startled response.

"Then do one of the other three and keep yourself pure before God and your wife," I said.

We talked some more, prayed together, and the conversation ended. I remembered when something similar had happened to a friend in a real estate office and he had fired the woman, but saved his manhood. I never heard from Ted again, but months later I learned that he had left that job and had taken another somewhere else.

Too often men blame themselves for their impure thought life, when in reality they are merely being influenced by the spirit of others — as Ted was. This is sufficient reason to be steeped in the Word of God and daily saturated with God's Spirit as a bulwark against the spirits which seek to infiltrate our minds and spirits.

In today's parlance we would call Ted's experience "picking up vibes." "Vibrations of the spirit" is how the communication of spirit to spirit is described by metaphysical teachers today. Singles just call it "chemistry."

God calls it "a witness in the Spirit."

A man who feels pure in his spirit each morning as he prays with an honest heart before God, but who feels spiritually disturbed or depleted by the time he gets to his office, needs to take a serious look at his environment. Something in it could be affecting his spiritual state. The problem may be, for example, a billboard he passes each day on his way to work without giving any thought to its message or imagery. Even though that billboard may not be blatant enough to attract his conscious attention, subliminally it may be suggestive or provocative enough to affect his spirit without his even realizing it.

The communication of the spirit of that billboard, and the men who devised it, is creating a serious problem for him. It is not coming from his spirit, but from theirs. Nevertheless, he is affected by it, needs to realize it, then do something about it.

"Flee also youthful lusts,"[3] is a good exhortation from God's Word. Those seducing spirits from the communication of others are real.

Men need to ask God to help them become aware of the spiritual influences which surround them in their daily lives and routines. Communication of the spirit is powerful and can be used as a tool of the enemy. We must be on guard against it and know how to recognize and handle it effectively. When our spirits are cleansed and pure, then we can communicate freely from our hearts to the rest of the world around us.

But then there is the man whose spirit is pure before God, but who finds that, even so, he does not love his wife. It happens.

67

Gary was such a man. He was a missionary to Taiwan. He had a wife, a small child, a new-born baby, and a marriage that was in danger of collapse. He knew that with the failure of his marriage, his missionary duty — and probably his ministerial relationship to his denomination — would be terminated. With what seemed to him to be his whole life and career on the line, he went to God in honesty and humility.

The truth was, there was no love between him and his wife. The only reason they were still together was because they were both Christians and missionaries. To them, the thought of divorce was anathema.

Gary continued to seek God over the situation. His intensity increased over the days and weeks. It was not uncommon for him to read his Bible and pray long after his wife had gone to bed. He needed help. He admitted it.

One night while meditating and continuing to wait on God for help, the words "love your wife" came alive in his mind and heart. It was as though God had spoken with an audible voice.

Gary began to meditate on what the Lord had meant when "love your wife" had burned into his mind. He searched the Scriptures about the subject and came to the one that says, "Husbands, love your wives, even as Christ also loved the church, and gave himself for it."[4]

Pondering those words, mulling them over and over in his mind, Gary went through the days seeking for an answer. Then one night when their baby cried, Gary did something new. Instead of lying in bed pretending to be asleep, and guiltily watching his wife as she rose to give the child a bottle, Gary told his wife to stay in bed and he would take care of the baby.

Nightly, Gary became the one to care for the baby while his wife slept.

After they had entertained some friends one day, Gary told his wife to go ahead and tend to the children, and he would take care of the kitchen duties.

After several weeks, Gary noticed a change in his wife. There was a softening, a mellowing, a warmth he hadn't seen for so long he had forgotten it was there. He noticed that she smiled at him more often, and that there were no more sharp cutting comments between them.

"'Man, when I learned to love by giving myself, it changed my life. When I changed, she changed. Today my wife and I have a marriage that must be in the top one percent of all the best marriages in the world,'' is the way Gary described it to me.

Gary cleansed his spirit, then let his gestures confirm his words, and soon God had worked a miracle of love in his married life. Gestures meant more than words.

Changing diapers at 3:00 a.m. may be hard, but it is much easier than divorce.

"A man's heart determines his speech,"[5] is what Proverbs says. But a man's actions determine his affection.

If you want to change your emotions, change your actions. Emotions follow actions, just as day follows night. When the emotions of love are not there, just begin to act on what is right and let God take care of the rest.

Why should your marriage be O.K.? *To glorify God!* There is no better reason. It's enough of a reason for a man to do whatever is necessary so God can get the glory.

God gets no glory from divorce. There is none.

My wife, Nancy, and I were strolling through a resort area on a quiet, lazy spring afternoon, holding hands and enjoying being together. I gave her hand an affectionate squeeze — a slight thing — but she glanced at me out of the corner of her eye and gave me a slow, languid, loving smile. Not a word was spoken. The spirit and gestures said it all.

The spirit in which we communicate seals all we say and do.

God's love without Calvary would be so meaningless.

A man's love without communication is so worthless.

Be free to communicate. Cleanse your spirit with God's Word, then release your spirit with your words. Confirm your words with your gestures.

Live your manhood to the fullest.

Learn to communicate by word, gesture, and spirit.

PART II:
SEX

9

THE SACREDNESS OF SEX

While I was in Washington, D.C., preparing for our National Christian Men's Event, an investigative reporter came to interview me. Since everything in that city revolves around politics, he was curious about my organization.

"What is the name of your political action committee?" he asked me.

"What are you talking about?" I asked.

"Don't you talk to men all over the country about sex?"

"That's a part of what we talk about."

"Well, what are you doing about incest, abortion, and other such matters of concern?"

"I'm commanding men to be virgins when they marry, and to be faithful to their wives after marriage," I said bluntly. "If men do that, you won't need political action committees or laws. Neither Congress nor the Supreme Court will ever be a substitute for obedience to God's Word."

"That's impossible!" he said.

"You obviously don't understand the Bible," I told him. "And you don't understand the power of God or else you wouldn't say that. I've watched literally thousands of men who have responded with alacrity, manliness, and real enthusiasm when they heard the truth. When men hear the truth, they respond to it like men."

It's true.

In this society filled with pornography on paper and screen, where lust is glorified, sex is cheap, marriage is portrayed as nothing but a problem, and living together is a solution, where a woman is viewed as nothing more than a body made to gratify a man's lust, in the midst of it all it is a thrill to see young men make decisions to come out of that culture and commit themselves to becoming champions for Christ.

So many marriages start wrong, stay wrong, and end wrong.

Much of this happens because men do not understand that sex is sacred.

In a society whose heroes are promiscuous, profane and pernicious, the influence on young people is damning.

Who teaches young men about sex?

In a recently published newspaper poll of 1,000 teenagers (about 48 percent of whom were boys), 38 percent of the youngsters were found to learn about sex ''on their own,'' 23 percent from friends, 20 percent at home, and 12 percent at school.

Only one boy in seven learns about sex at home, and there are not enough who learn about it at church to show up in the research data. Only 2 percent of those interviewed said they thought sex should be taught in school.

These same interviewees thought that a girl could not get pregnant the first time she had sex, that condoms ruin sexual pleasure, that oral copulation is not sex, and that masturbation is good. Fifty percent admitted they had already engaged in sex while still in high school.

The poll also estimated that an average of 9,230 suggestive comments or scenes representing sexual intercourse are shown on American television each year.

In not one instance has the Church been identified with teaching the truth concerning the sacredness of sex.

Scripture says, "The priest's lips should keep knowledge, and they (the people) should seek the law at his mouth: for he is the messenger of the Lord of hosts."[1]

Sex is the highest physical act of love between two people to show their union in spirit, which is a covenant relationship.

To understand this truth, it is necessary to understand God's covenant relationship with man. God's way of bringing man back to Himself in redemptive grace is revealed in His covenant plan.

That plan is seen in Abraham's relationship with God. "Abraham believed God," the Bible says, "and it was counted unto him for righteousness."[2] That act of faith brought Abraham into a covenant relationship with God.

By faith Abraham was brought into union with God in spirit. God worked in Abraham's heart by "circumcising" it, or putting away uncleanness from it. Their unity in faith was by communication in spirit.

There was no external evidence of what had happened except that Abram's name was changed to Abraham. God then commanded Abraham to be circumcised in body. Circumcision was to represent physically something which had transpired spiritually. It was something sacred to God and Abraham.

Circumcision was an external evidence of an internal work.

Circumcision was of the heart first, and of the flesh second. If it had not been of the heart first, then that of the flesh would have had no meaning.

The foreskin represented the uncleanness of a man's life. Circumcision (the cutting off and casting away of that foreskin) was symbolic of what had occurred when God cleansed the heart of man.

Circumcision is mentioned in Scripture as being of the heart, the lips, and other parts of the body besides the male reproductive organ. These scriptures were given as a sign to the people that they were to sanctify those parts of their bodies by having the impure, unclean, corrupt uses of them put away forever.

The practice of circumcision is found in society in various ways. Bankruptcy is a form of financial circumcision. It represents the putting away of a person's debts (or financial "uncleanness") so he can begin all over again as though he had never been encumbered or "soiled." God's principle of "jubilee" was the forerunner of this type of financial liberation.

Circumcision of the lips takes place when the profanity that is so profusely practiced is exorcised from a person's speech and a new righteousness fills his heart. Even minced oaths become intolerable in the lives of those deeply committed to God.

Circumcision involves the shedding of blood. All covenants based on blood require a mutual exchange of life. All freedom in life is based on blood.

Freedom from disease only comes by the sacrifice of blood. The lives of many people (and countless laboratory animals) had to be sacrificed in order for science to develop the vaccines that have freed us from the heavy toll of such diseases as polio and smallpox.

Freedom from political enslavement only comes by the sacrifice of blood. It was the offering up of the lives of hundreds of thousands of brave men and women that has enabled Americans to enjoy and preserve the political freedom we know today. Those crosses on the battlefields of this world are silent witnesses to the multitudes who have shed their life's blood that others might live free.

"Without shedding of blood is no remission,"[3] is the scriptural statement of the principle.

Circumcision was an external evidence of an internal work. It was a sign of a covenant relationship between man and God. That Old Testament practice was changed in the New Testament after Calvary.

No longer would the blood of bulls and goats suffice for God to put away the sins of Israel for another year. Now the blood (or the life, for the life is in the blood) of Christ was offered once and for all to take away the sins of man so there would be no further need of any sacrifice.

Circumcision of the heart would always be necessary for faith in God, but the external evidences of what occurs in the heart would be altered.

Water baptism became the sign of the new covenant relationship.

It was, and is, deeply significant to a life of faith. Mark wrote that it was a requirement for a life of obedience through faith. It wasn't something that could be regarded with a "take-it-or-leave-it" attitude; it was not to be entered lightly nor totally ignored.

Baptism was, and is, an act of identification with Jesus Christ — His life, death, crucifixion, burial, resurrection and ascension. It reveals and testifies physically and openly before the world of what has happened spiritually and internally.

Water baptism is the believer's testimony that he has repented of his sinful life, has been crucified with Christ (has died to sin), has been buried with Him (the old nature is dead), and has been raised with Him to live forever in resurrection life. The symbolism of baptism is only meaningful if the heart and soul have first experienced the New Birth. It is meaningless without it.

God didn't call anyone to live a "crucified life," but rather a "resurrected life." If we were called to live a crucified life, then whoever baptized us would have left us at the bottom of the tank, pool, river or ocean! God's purpose in sending Christ was "that they (we) might have life, and that they (we) might have it more abundantly."[4]

What does all of this have to do with sex? If you don't know that God wants you to have an abundant life, then why bother reading about how He created sex! It is for our good, not our harm!

Circumcision and water baptism are both signs of a covenant relationship. Circumcision was, and water baptism is, an external evidence of an internal work.

Sex is also an external evidence of an internal work.

When two people are joined together in marriage, they become "one flesh."[5] Their spirits become united, and they enter into a relationship with each other through faith. The exchange of their vows is a confession of faith that they have entered into a covenant relationship in marriage, and sex is the physical evidence of it.

Marriage is a covenant relationship.

God's Word says, "Marriage is honourable in all, and the bed undefiled."[6]

Sex is the sign of a covenant relationship between a man and a woman.

The covenant is why God gave sex only to those who are married.

Sex wasn't made for lusting and getting. It was made for loving and giving.

Engaging in any sex act outside of marriage is a sin. Engaging in sex when single is called fornication. If indulged in with a member of the opposite sex other than one's marriage partner, or with one who is in a covenant with another partner, it is called adultery. Sex between two people of the same sex is called homosexuality or (if both partners are female) lesbianism. Sex with an animal is called bestiality. All of these are referred to in the Bible as sin.

Where two people have not entered into the sacred covenant of marriage, there is to be no sex between them.

Sex was given as an act of love, not lust.

Lust is perverted love.

Love desires to satisfy others, even at the expense of self.

Lust desires to gratify self, even at the expense of others.

Sex was made for giving.

Love gives, lust gets.

When a married man engages in an intimate sexual relationship with his wife and while engaged is imagining he is having sex with another person, he is only practicing vaginal masturbation. Actually he is committing adultery in his heart. There is no communciation between that man and woman in spirit, only in the flesh.

Someone once asked me, ''Isn't it dishonoring to think that sex can be regarded as sacred?''

Hey — Who do you think created sex?

The devil didn't.

Satan is not a creator; he is a counterfeiter, usurper, and thief. He will counterfeit, usurp or steal anything that God creates.

God creates, Satan counterfeits.

The joy of sex is knowing that you have entered into a holy, covenant relationship with the woman you love, and that God gladly has provided a joyous, exciting, physically pleasing act with which you seal your covenant. Each time you have sex with your wife, you are once again saying with every fiber of your being that you love her.

Sex with guilt is nothing like that at all.

Sex without guilt is the greatest pleasure a man will ever know.

Sex is sacred to a marriage!
Sex is for marriage.

10

THE GLORY OF VIRGINITY

There is a glory to virginity.

Virginity is part of the uniqueness with which God endowed both men and women in creation. Virginity is a glory both to men and women.

In this day and age, virginity is regarded as useless by much of the medical profession, as a shame to those with it, as a trophy to be won by "macho men," as an embarrassment to young ladies, and as a nuisance to incestuous parents.

To God and the godly, it is a glory.

God expects both men and women to be virgins when they marry — not just the women.

God has no double standards — man does, God doesn't.

It is my belief that the divorce rate in America is directly proportionate to the loss of virginity.

God's standard for virginity before marriage was for a divine purpose. Men need to understand the truth concerning virginity, and fathers need to know why God holds them responsible for their virginal daughters.

In Deuteronomy 22:13-21, God is very explicit in His instructions concerning the newlywed couple. In the Jewish culture, there was a distinct manner in which newlyweds were to come together.

God gave explicit instructions on how to adjudicate the matter if the man wanted an annulment on the grounds that his bride was not a virgin when he married her. The evidence of the purity of the woman was to be found in her "tokens of virginity" — that is, the presence of blood on the marital bedclothes.

The parents of the bride were to furnish the newlyweds with a set of "bedclothes" for the couple's first night of marriage and their initial act of sexual intercourse.

After their first night together, if the man brought a charge against his new bride that he found her not a virgin, then the parents of the bride were to obtain the bedclothes used that night, and spread them before the elders of the city to give evidence concerning their daughter's "tokens of virginity."

If the tokens were found, it was evidence that the man had lied in an attempt to gain an annulment. He was attempting to defraud his new bride and her parents.

His charge, if false, was a slander against a "virgin of Israel," and incurred a severe penalty. First, the husband was to pay the parents of the bride a fine for bringing a false charge against their daughter. Second, he would have to continue the marriage with never an opportunity for divorce. He was married to the woman for life.

This meant that she could not be put away and made to fend for herself, hoping to find someone who would take her as a once-divorced woman to be a wife again. The man's penalty was the responsibility to provide and care for the woman all her life.

But, if his charge was true — if the woman was not a virgin, though representing herself to be — then the husband was given the annulment he desired. Her penalty for defrauding her parents and husband was to be brought before the people of the city and be stoned.

She had "wrought folly in Israel, to play the whore in her father's house,"[1] by losing her virginity while still living at home, and the penalty was death.

God expected both the man and the woman to be virgins at the time of their marriage. It is possible to prove the virginity of a woman, but not the virginity of a man. The man's word was to be reliable. The woman has the power of sex, the ability to give or keep it. It was assumed that if she had not been raped or had not lost her virginity through forcible sexual assault, then she had voluntarily submitted to sexual intercourse before marriage — which was contrary to God's commandment.

Before continuing, let me point out something to you as a man. Men do not realize the penalty or curse that comes from lying about or slandering a woman. A man who, after a date, brags about his "conquest," when in reality there was none, slanders a woman and causes her the loss of her reputation. Men who do this are subject to the judgment of God.

I warn you against making any statement of untruth regarding a woman's virtue. In fact, if you are guilty of having done it, I command you to repent. Ask God to forgive you of your sin of slander. You have raised up a slander against God's handmaiden and it will not go unpunished.

When I mentioned this to a group of college men, their leader told me it answered his question as to why there seemed to be such a curse on campus, especially in some men's "frat houses." You cannot violate God's commandments, or even His children, and not expect His judgment.

Another factor in this dispute between a husband and wife about her virginity was the severity of the punishment that was meted out to the guilty parties. Note that the law stated: "So shalt thou put evil away from among you (Israel)."[2] The punishment for all to see was done to bring the "fear of the Lord"[3] upon all of Israel.

Think of what would happen to our country today if there was a law enacted that required a man to take care of, for life, every woman whose virginity he had taken, and that required a woman's life if she was not a virgin when she married.

We'd have a financial crisis, for one thing. Our courtrooms and doctors' offices would be full of people arguing about the modern-day equivalents of the "tokens of virginity." Young people would certainly think twice before losing their virginity.

The consequences of fraud were meant by God to bring the "fear of the Lord" upon Israel. "The fear of the Lord is the beginning of wisdom,"[4] says the Bible, and the beginning of wisdom is to depart from evil. The fear of the Lord is required to begin to be wise.

Scripture states that in the early Church when the disciples were "walking in the fear of the Lord, and in the comfort of the Holy Ghost,"[5] multitudes were added to the Church. The fear of the Lord is not an awesome dread of God, but an awe-inspired reverence that leads to a departure from evil.

Today much of the Church tends to walk only in the comfort of the Holy Ghost and ignores the fear of the Lord. As a result, much of the world lives in lasciviousness of life. *Lasciviousness* literally means "living without restraint." The world only knows restraint from the power of the Spirit. The Church gives it by walking in the fear of the Lord. The Church can't indulge in lasciviousness to any degree and still expect God to bless and empower it. Where is the fear of the Lord?

God is not winking at sin.

The rise and fall of the fear of the Lord in the life of believers has a direct bearing on the rise and fall of unrighteousness in our communities and nation. The lack of the fear of the Lord in the Church today is cause for much of the rise of evil in the world.

Historically, whenever great fear of the Lord was upon the Church, it translated into great evangelism in the community. Conviction of sin can't occur where sin is lightly regarded or indulged in by church members.

Where the Church is walking in the strength of the fear of the Lord, there is a restraint from doing evil in society.

Don't think for a minute that the way you live as an individual has no effect on this world — it certainly does. By your relationship to God, you are directly influencing what happens in this world.

Public denunciation of sin is predicated on private renunciation.

God wanted Israel to walk in the fear of the Lord that they might have an influence on all the nations of the world. He wanted to reveal Himself to the world through Israel. For Him to be able to do that, they needed to walk both in the comfort of His presence, and in reverence before Him.

Every man who renounces sins makes an impact on the world around him.

The world stands up and takes notice of the man who walks in the fear of the Lord.

The nation that fears the Lord makes an impact on the world. To the degree that the nation loses its fear of the Lord, it will lose its influence in the world.

The heavy penalty laid upon those guilty of sexual fraud was imposed in an attempt to "put away sin" directly and to bring the fear of the Lord upon the rest of the nation to restrain them from evil.

The act of marriage, sex, is a holy act.

God still expects His people to respond to the covenant He has provided for them with the fear of the Lord in their hearts. Marriage is a covenant relationship. The covenant is a blood covenant.

When the couple on their wedding night engage in their first act of intimate sexual intercourse, and her hymen is penetrated, it causes the shedding of blood and that blood then becomes the "tokens of her virginity."

When the hymen of the bride is penetrated, causing the shedding of blood, and that blood flows over the man's penis, it is a sign before God that the man and woman have entered into a sacred covenant relationship in marriage through the shedding of blood. That shed blood is symbolic of the sacred covenant relationship with God which is entered into through the shedding of Christ's blood.

Initial sex is a sign of a blood covenant.

Virginity is a glory.

If you are a virgin, your virginity is a glory to you.

What a way to start a marriage, with a blood covenant recognized by you, God, and your new wife. Think of it!

Your wedding night — you and your wife together in the honeymoon suite of the hotel — you in your blue silk pajamas, and her in the beautiful white peignoir. You toast each other with sparkling catawba, smile lovingly and intimately at each other. . .

Then, taking her in your arms, you guide her to the bed, and tell her, "Sweetheart, I love you. God gave to me the 'glory of virginity' as part of my manhood. Tonight, I share it with you, the greatest gift I can give to you as an act of my true love for you. I want our marriage to be a sacred covenant in God, and our sex to be the sign of that covenant."

Clean.

Pure.

Holy.

Good.

Righteous.

Godly.

Manly.

Don't let some cheap, tawdry relationship in the back of a van, or at a cheap motel, or on a sandy beach blanket, or in hushed whispers in the living room, rob you of the greatest moment of your life!

"Present your bodies a living sacrifice, holy, acceptable unto God, which is your reasonable service,"[6] is what the Bible says. Yes, it is reasonable! It makes good sense!

Once you have presented your body to God as a living sacrifice, holy, acceptable unto the Lord, which is your reasonable service, then hold it in that "glory" so you will be able to present it to your wife in the same way — on your wedding night — holy and acceptable to her — which is your reasonable service.

God is calling you to excellence.

Are you single and having problems honoring God with purity in mind or body? Are you willing to admit that you want to be a man of excellence, not ashamed of your identification with Christ, a man who knows what is right and is not afraid to admit it, a man who will respond to the call for excellence of life?

The spirit and glory of virginity are yours.

Or are you no longer a virgin and have just realized what you have lost and would desire to have it back? You may not get it back physically, but you can mentally, emotionally, and spiritually. God will restore the spirit and glory of it to your life if you ask Him.

Or are you married — and now realize you lost the glory of your virginity the wrong way — and you would like to have the spirit and glory of it restored to your life to renew your relationship with your wife? Again, you may not have it back physically, but you can certainly have the spirit of it back mentally and spiritually. It will change your whole attitude toward your wife, your relationship to her, and will give you a new, fresh love for her.

Or are you a divorced person or a widower who wants to remarry and do it the right way? You too can experience it from God.

If you are married, you and your wife can be restored in your spirits so you can approach your marriage bed with a new attitude, one of thankfulness and reverence for the covenant God has provided for you.

If you desire the spirit and glory of virginity in your life, and you are not ashamed to admit you want your life to be a glory to God, then without any embarrassment, pray this prayer with me.

"Father, in the Name of Jesus, my Lord and Savior, I come to You now, to present my body, holy, acceptable to You, which is my reasonable service. By faith I receive the Holy Spirit's quickening power in my life to renew within me the spirit and the glory of virginity. In the spirit of virginity, I present my body, holy and acceptable, to that person to whom I will marry (or to whom I am married), which is my reasonable service. I accept Your provision for this covenant relationship in my life and thank You for it. Amen."

Excellent.

Receive that renewing power in your life and the glory that is yours through Christ.

The glory of virginity is yours today.

11
THE PRINCIPLE OF RELEASE

I was in my hotel room when the phone rang. It was the grandmother of the little eight-year-old girl I had prayed with the night before.

During the course of the meeting that night, I was impressed to pray for women who had been abused. The first time I did that, the response was so phenomenal that I had been careful not to repeat it unless definitely impressed to do so.

One out of every four women has been abused or sexually assaulted by some man during her girlhood. These women need healing from the emotional hurt. For most of them, therapy is not even considered. The majority of these victims simply stuff the experience into the back of their minds hoping never to remember it again — only to find it is a stumbling block to the real intimacy, openness, and vulnerability of genuine love.

Therefore, it is not strange that the Lord would want to minister to these women, and to do it through a man. By man came the offense, by man comes the release.

The principle of release (my terminology) is one of the most powerful Jesus gives the believer. He said to His disciples, ''Receive ye the Holy Ghost: Whose soever sins ye remit, they are remitted unto them; and whose soever sins ye retain, they are retained.''[1]

If you forgive anyone his sins, they are forgiven (released), and if you do not forgive, they are not forgiven (released). You retain what you do not release.

This is how sins are passed from generation to generation. Sons who do not forgive the sins of their fathers retain them and make the same mistakes with their sons. Time after time in meetings when I have taught this principle, men have finally understood why they do what they do. Literally hundreds of men have stood and openly attested to the fact that they are making the same mistakes with their sons that their fathers made with them.

But the wonderful thing is that Jesus made a way to release the mistakes, errors, and sins out of our lives. By receiving the power of the Holy Spirit and forgiving as God forgives, they are released from our lives. We can live free from the mistakes of the past.

That night when the grandmother stood with her granddaughter and the other ladies, I did what I normally do at that time. I stood before those women in the place of the man, or men, who had hurt, abused, violated, or misused them, and I asked them to forgive me in his stead. It is always a most moving moment in their lives.

After asking them to forgive, it is common for me then to pray with them, often leading them in a prayer of release. A simple prayer, but oh so powerful, as the Spirit of God quickens the hearts, minds, and spirits of those who pray it.

The grandmother on the phone told me what happened after the meeting when she took her granddaughter home. The precious little eight-year-old had been raped when she was six. The emotional trauma still bothered her at times, so she was often left with her grandmother instead of a babysitter while the mother worked.

"I took my granddaughter home last night and put her to bed," the grandmother reported. "After I tucked her in, before I prayed for her, I asked her what Jesus had done for her that night.

"She looked at me and said, 'Grandma, Jesus made me feel just like I did before it ever happened.' "

God can do more in one touch of His Spirit than the whole world can do in all our lifetimes put together.

For some women, it takes longer to let it all out because of the wall of bitterness, regret, resentment, and even hatred that has built up over the years. For others, the years just add momentum once the person makes the decision to forgive, and it all comes pouring out in a torrent as the Spirit of God unlocks what has been bound up for so long.

Many women suffer the consequences of a man's sin.

Consider this letter:

"Dear Dr. Cole:

"I hate men. My first and real father was an alcoholic. He physically abused my mother, sister, and me. My stepfather has physically abused me and my sister since we were eleven years old. To this day, I won't stay in the same room with him — it still happens.

"No, my mother doesn't know. I'm afraid to tell her, she won't believe me; and my sister said if I told Mom, she would deny it.

"My dad claims to be a Christian. It makes me want to vomit when I sit in the choir loft at church and have to look at him sitting there in the church singing. He makes me sick. I HATE HIM. I have tried to forgive him, and when I went and told him I had forgiven him, he just laughed at me and acted as if he hadn't done anything wrong.

"He's a member of the church. I have talked to the pastor about this; he says he doesn't feel he should approach him at this time. Why? Doesn't anyone care about me — my feelings?"

Jesus does.

Such cases are the very reason the Lord has called men like me to stand before women "in His stead" so they can be freed from what we men have done to them. It is what I call the ministry of the principle of release.

Negative sexual experiences like this one don't just fade away. Unless they are dealt with, they become lodged deep within the person and cause all kinds of problems later on in life. Any pastor, psychologist or social worker who has done any amount of personal counseling will tell you that. People sometimes go through life with the memory of that nagging, unfinished business deep inside their spirit. That's why they never fully experience the joy of the Lord in their sex life.

I sat in my office one day with a married couple who were in constant turmoil. Regardless of how much they talked things out, and how many hours of counseling they received, their marriage remained an absolute mess.

Finally, in a counseling session which turned out to be our last, on a sudden impulse I asked the two of them, "Did you have premarital sex together?" Rather sheepishly they admitted that they had. Then the wife began to cry. Then weep. Her husband and I sat there absolutely amazed at how much emotion welled up in her over this one incident that had taken place years before.

As she cried, I turned to her husband and asked him, "Have you ever asked her to forgive you for causing her to lose her virginity before you were married?"

His reply, of course, was that he had not.

"This would be a good time, son, to do it," I said.

That couple never had to come to see me again. The strife was gone. Peace began to reign in their lives and home, because of the principle of release.

In a recent meeting in which this truth was presented, a woman came to me with a joyful heart. "I could never figure out why I never felt good enough to be a wife or mother, until I heard the truth about the principle of release. My virginity was taken from me when I was five, and I just realized it was the reason I could never feel deserving. I always felt like I was less than a real woman. Tonight I forgave the man who did it, and for the first time in my life I consider myself to be a real woman."

A pastor called me to tell me what had happened to a lady in his congregation. When she was sixteen years old, she was gang raped by six men in a van. They were ready to kill her when a police car was spotted driving by, and instead they threw her unmercifully out of the van and sped away.

Now, years later, she was a beautiful wife and mother of three children. Inside though, all her life, she had ached from the trauma inflicted upon her by those ungodly, perverse attackers. She still battled the feelings of shame, hate, guilt, and uncleanness which had been thrust upon her when her virginity was so violently stolen from her.

However, after hearing the principle and praying the prayer of release, she called her pastor to give him the wonderfully good news that she had finally been healed of that nightmare. The Spirit of Christ had renewed her mind, spirit, and body.

She told her pastor that for the first time in her life she actually, physically, desired her husband. She was free. Free to love.

It's not just women, though; men have suffered the same.

In San Antonio after I had prayed with abused women, a man spoke up loudly before the entire audience, "What about us men?" It startled everyone, and I honestly replied, "I'm sorry, it just never occurred to me to include the men. If you need help, let me pray with you now."

He was a schoolteacher. He had been violated as a boy by his own father and brother. Because of it, he battled a spirit of homosexuality. He desired a normal heterosexual life, but because of what he had suffered as a boy, he thought it never would — or could — be for him.

But he too was released.

Notice though, that our Lord commanded, "Receive ye the Holy Ghost," before He gave the principle of release. To forgive as God forgives, it must be done in the power of His Spirit. It cannot be done as a willful human exercise of fleshly faith. Jesus knew what we needed, and He prayed the Father to send His own Spirit into our hearts via the New Birth so we could know His power, grace and truth, and be able to live our lives in Him.

If you have an attitude about sex that does not come from the Lord, you need to find out where that attitude comes from and get it out of your life. Many times wrong attitudes about sex are a holdover from some past experience. God is there for you. He wants to release you from your past and lead you into a new future.

Do you need release? Are there sins that have been committed against you that need to be erased from your mind and spirit? Have you desired to be free? Are you still carrying the sins of others because you have never had anyone minister this word to you? Then let me pray with you — here — now.

First, let me take the place of the man (or woman) who has violated you, offended you, corrupted you, and ask you to forgive me in their stead. They will probably never be able to say it — but I can do it for them.

Forgive me. If you are a woman, forgive what we men have done to you.

Now let me pray with you. Pray this prayer with me.

"God, my Father, I come to You now in accordance with Your Word to believe and receive the healing virtue of Jesus Christ into my life. By faith I receive Your Spirit in quickening power into my life. By the authority of Your Word, and the ability of Your Spirit, I now forgive that person and what was done to me. I release it right out of my life. And now — by faith — I receive Your healing virtue to restore in my life what was stolen from me. Amen.''

Now, if you have been the one who abused, misused, or violated another person or persons, and you are not able to go and apologize for your actions directly, God will also release you from the bondage of that sin. Pray the same prayer, but instead of your forgiving someone else, ask God to forgive you for your wrongdoing. Then receive by faith your healing from the scars of your own sins.

Pray this prayer. Mean it.

Receive your release from the Lord.

He said it. He will do it.

Be free.

12

GOD MADE SEX GOOD

Thus far we have written about men and their character. We have said that there are three basic common problem areas between a man and a woman: communication, sex and money. There are only three methods of communciation known to man: words, gesture and spirit. Virginity is God-given, and a glory, not something to be shunned or shamed by. There is a principle of release that Jesus Christ has given us for our freedom from the sins committed against us.

We have talked about the sacredness of sex, in that it is a sign of a covenant relationship between a man and a woman. Not bad.

But, let's continue the subject of sex in this book with a simple statement.

God made sex good!

As long as I live I shall never forget the day in a seminar at a Holiday Inn in Irving, Texas, when I made that statement and three hundred Texans all shouted, "Amen!"

All I could think of was three hundred wives calling me, wanting to know what under God's heaven I had said to their husbands.

Yet, the truth is that God made sex good, made it to be the most desirable thing for a man in relationship to a woman so the earth would be replenished, or repopulated, and thus fulfill God's command. God made sex good so that man would not feel forced to replenish the earth. He also made it good for man's pleasure because He loved the man.

Sex is not something to be ashamed of, avoided, denied or secretly lusted after. It is something lovely, good, holy, decent and in keeping with the covenant relationship between a man and wife.

In creation, God created the entire earth in the positive.

Man through sin recreated it in the negative.

Sin always promises to serve and please, but only desires to enslave and dominate. That's true of alcohol, drugs, pornography, greed, jealousy, and every other sin of the flesh and spirit.

God creates, Satan counterfeits.

The corner barroom is a counterfeit church. The bartender is the pastor, people go in to find fellowship, get counsel, and are filled with the spirit(s).

There is a freedom that comes from love, but lust gives a heavy burden.

Love is satisfying, lust is insatiable.

Just as hell is never satisfied, neither is the lust of the flesh. Lust is degenerative. From fantasies, sexual lust descends in its unbridled thirst to sado-masochism, then to bestiality, and finally to murder itself. Over 50,000 murders per year occur in America through sexual deviation.

The latest serial murderer I've read about was arrested for thirty-seven murders, all of them committed because of the sexual deviation and perversion of the accused.

There is no joy in lust. Lust is a counterfeit of love.

Prayer produces intimacy, but pornography is a substitute for prayer. Pornography promises to serve and please, but only enslaves and dominates. One psychologist stated that it takes four to five years of therapy to rid patients of sexual addictions. God can do it better.

The mores of society are imposing themselves on the Church, instead of the Church establishing the mores of society. Rather than be embarrassed by, criticize, or find fault with the men who are openly contending for righteousness in our society, we need to thank God for them, pray for them, and stand with them.

Pornography has made oral sex popular with the lustful, and a problem for the loving. A pastor asked me to speak at a women's luncheon, and then gave the ladies slips of paper on which to write their questions for me to answer. Eight out of ten questions were, ''What do you say about oral sex?''

A woman called our office asking for help because her husband had put her out of the house when she refused to engage in oral sex. She wanted to know what the Bible said about it.

The fact is, the Bible says nothing about it directly.

However, the Bible says plenty about love and sex.

Just as God did not force man to procreate, but instead made sex an enjoyable act that man would desire, so the man must treat his wife — not forcing anything on her but making the sex act enjoyable so she will desire it. The sexual union is directly related to a man's loving his wife even as Christ also loved the Church. Any man who *forces* his wife to engage in sexual acts *of any kind* is operating out of lust, not love.

One man wrote that he and his wife didn't have any problems, except one — she didn't want to have oral sex. He was wrong. He was blind to the real problems they had. The disagreement about oral sex was not ''his only problem,'' it was an indication and outgrowth of more serious underlying problems. Dealing with surface issues will never clear up deep-seated hurts, attitudes and beliefs.

If people were more educated concerning God's view of sex, the sacredness of the covenant, and if they had more fear of the Lord in their lives, there would not be a need to address these concerns.

"Whatsoever is not of faith is sin,"[1] is what scripture says.

Any time a man forces his wife to do something contrary to her consecration, and coerces her to do something outside of faith, it is sin. There is generally a basic attitude of lust versus love in the argument.

But here is a letter which reveals what happens when a man meets God.

"I praise God for the mighty work He has done and is doing through you, Brother Cole! My husband Rick attended the seminar you held in Chicago, and I had to write and tell you what the Lord has done.

"We had been married for about ten years. The first couple of years we were too dumb to know we had problems, and during the next four years our marriage relationship deteriorated until our family life had become almost unbearable. I thought I knew the Lord, but I finally was scared enough to get serious about straightening out my relationship with the Lord Jesus. And I began to pray, only with a 'can't-You-do-anything-about-this-jerk-I'm-living-with' attitude.

"Well, one night, while I was reading the Bible, I read Ephesians 5:22-24. Something (Someone, really) deep inside me said, 'This is for you.' I thought, 'Oh, no it's not,' and tried to keep right on reading. 'Far be it from me to submit to a man who's into drugs and alcohol, and doesn't even know You, Lord!' I thought. But that 'something' deep inside said gently, 'If you don't, you're a hypocrite.'

"I wrestled with that for weeks. Every scripture I read convicted me on the subject — everything in the circumstances seemed to prove that it would be the most foolish decision possible. My daughter was still breast-feeding, we had no money, Rick was leaving us 'for good' about twice a month, and was angry because I wouldn't smoke dope with him and his friends. But the conviction continued. My heart still reads Matthew 5:47 like this, 'And if you submit to Christ-like husbands only, what do you more than others?'

"Finally, I did submit to God *and* my husband, and got busy seeking God for what He wanted *me* to be — as a wife and otherwise. I found (under the Lord's guidance) that I was so blind, and so faulty in the heart department that I had *no business* thinking about what anyone did or didn't do — in particular, what my husband did or didn't do.

"To make an already long story short(er), the Lord went through both our lives, our marriage, our home, everything, so fast and in such power that my husband was saved, empowered by the Holy Spirit, and his drug-doing friends ran for the hills. The Lord found us a house, we stopped striving with each other, started having people in our home to study the Bible, and no one could believe we were the same two people.

"But there were a few stubborn problems: There were still tensions in our sex life; I still had a nagging sense of unforgiveness against alcoholics; my husband still felt guilty about all he had done, even though he knew God had forgiven him and he was dead to the things he had done before; and (in part because of these things, he tells me now) he hadn't taken his position as the spiritual head of the house.

"Now by this time I knew that God and Rick could settle any problem without me poking my nose in it, so I gave the care of our sex life over to God, and concentrated on working for Him, loving my husband, and keeping my own self in line.

"And to tell you the truth, after what we had been through, I would have been perfectly satisfied to live with those things. Outwardly there was no sign of trouble, and we were both growing steadily. I was so grateful to our Lord Jesus because of the change from marital disaster to a loving and relatively peaceful home, that I'd have *gladly* lived with the seemingly small things in our lives for any length of time.

"Then, one night, a brother in the Lord came to a home Bible study we were having and told Rick about your seminar the next day. He went, and when he got home that Saturday afternoon, I could hardly believe I was talking to the same man! He asked my forgiveness for not taking the spiritual leadership in our family and home Bible study meeting, and *took it*. He shared the principle of 'release' in forgiveness he had learned from you; I got on my knees and today I am free from the root of bitterness and unforgiveness against alcoholics. Rick is free from his left-over guilt about the things his former self had done, and new power began to flow through our lives.

"Brother Cole, that was enough to keep me shouting the Lordship of Jesus Christ with fresh joy, and turning handsprings for a long, long time to come. But there's more.

"You spoke to the men about oral sex. That problem was the very specific one that I had turned over to the Lord, and then only with insecurity. (I wasn't too sure that Jesus was in the business of straightening out people's sex lives — I'd never heard much about it. But I reasoned that He did, after all, create it — He's infinitely compassionate, and He does love us, so I banked on that and turned it over anyhow.) I had not said one word about it, not to my husband or anyone else, except to Jesus.

"Sir, when my husband walked in and told me what had been said, and that he had asked the Lord's forgiveness, and was now asking mine, the infinite love of the Lord Jesus Christ was so real to me I'd have been on my knees worshipping Him in that same instant, had I not been caught up in my husband's arms."

The seminar she was referring to was one of our "men only" meetings where I simply told the men that whatever is not of faith is sin, and the marriage bed is undefiled. The Holy Spirit is our teacher, the Bible says, and I let the Holy Spirit minister to the men individually after I presented the basic Biblical truths. This man accepted what God ministered to his heart and reaped a huge reward in his relationship with his wife. But the problem today is that often men are trained merely to hear sermons, not to study the Word of God or heed His "still small voice" in their hearts.

But notice in this woman's letter where the change began.

It always begins in us.

Any change you desire in someone else must begin in you. If your wife has seemed to be the wrong one, and you the right one, humble yourself before the Lord merely to do what He asks you to do in faith, believing that He will take care of the rest.

Impatience is the tool of the flesh, misunderstanding is the tool of the devil.

For your sake, your wife's sake, your children's sake, for God's sake — be the man God created you to be. Don't be a counterfeit. Be genuine. Be real.

Be a man.

The contradiction in men's lives is never so apparent as when they walk into the bedroom at night with the attitude, "Wait here, Jesus, I'll be back in the morning."

The Holy of Holies is now tabernacled in the heart of man. It's why Jesus could promise, "I will never leave thee, nor forsake thee."[2] His Spirit indwells you every moment of every day, at all times working for your good. God is with you in the workroom, boardroom, kitchen, and bedroom.

Sure, there are some women as addicted to lust even as men, and they need the same renewing of the spirit of the mind that a man does. Sure, there are some women who consider their ability to seduce a man as evidence of their being a conqueror of him. Sure, there are women who are frigid.

Many women have problems with sex, not because they don't recognize it as a legitimate ministry of theirs to their husband, but because of his lusts.

One of the aspects of the man's ministry as prophet, priest and king is the ability to meet his wife's needs. Because a husband doesn't listen, a wife won't talk — about her problems — to him. But she will find someone who will listen, and when she does, she will often transfer her affection. That spells trouble.

That is why it is so important to understand the methods of communicating. Listening is the basic part of communication. You don't make a success in life because of your ability to speak, but because of your ability to listen.

Yes, God made sex good.

Righteousness makes it good.

Every man needs to have his heart and mind circumcised from uncleanness, to put away the impurities, and then to accept the riches of what is godly, pure and holy.

Sometimes it takes more than one effort to achieve excellence. That's why I wrote in the book COURAGE: A Book for Champions that "champions are not men who never fail, but men who never quit."

Like any investment, it will take time to see the results. Whereas the weak, fearful man gives up before the return comes in, a man who truly loves God will remain faithful until he reaps a harvest.

13

THE CIRCUMCISED MARRIAGE

When Bill called, I was busy preparing for a very important presentation at a bookseller's convention. The days were busy and long, and the nights were too short. Bill and his wife needed counsel, he said, and wanted to know if they could meet with me.

The answer was obviously, "No." No way.

Yet as I was explaining to Bill on the phone the reasons why it was impossible for me to meet with him and his wife at this time, I found myself telling him that I'd meet them late that night. Little did I know God wanted to do something in their lives that would profoundly change them, and through their experience, the lives of thousands of others.

"We've been married thirty years, yet there is something missing in our marriage," Bill began as he and Jan sat on the couch in my hotel room that night. "There's no romance. Sex is almost non-existent. We really need help. We believe God told us to come to you."

If it was true that God thought I could help, I was grateful, but at the moment I didn't know if Bill really knew what he was talking about. Events would prove that he did.

Bill proceeded to tell me that he was 52 years old, Jan was 51, and that after thirty years together they were convinced it was a miracle their marriage had lasted as long as it had. After they were first married, she had told him that she wasn't able to have children. His angry response had been, "If that's the case, then there's no need to have sex."

But they did, though it was far from what either of them desired, wanted, or imagined it could and should be. Bill went on to tell of the next thirty years of intermittent heartache, occasional tragedy, distress, pain, sorrow, and just enough affection interspersed throughout to keep the marriage together.

It was a long story, and by the ease with which he related to me the details, I could tell they had talked it over and thought it over time and time again. I decided to interrupt Bill and just get the basics instead of the details.

"Do you want this marriage to work?" I asked.

Bill looked at his wife, and they turned to me and each said, "Yes."

"Do you love each other?"

"We don't know," was their honest answer.

"Have you been faithful to each other?"

"I've looked over the fence a few times, and probably he has too, but we haven't done anything," Jan said, and Bill nodded in agreement.

"But you don't know if you love each other?"

"All I know," said Bill, "is that through it all, she is still my best friend."

That statement said a lot to me about their situation. It was classic evidence of the truth that what holds a marriage together is not romance, but friendship. A marriage union needs both, but it can survive on the basis of friendship alone without romance. Few ever survive with only the romance and no friendship. Hollywood romance magazines revealing the constant change in marital relationships among celebrities illustrate the point.

A young man needs to know how to be a friend to a girl, in order to know how to be a husband to a woman.

Exotic and erotic moments don't last a lifetime, friendship does. You can't build a life on memories.

In the absence of true friendship, between the times of romance, the void can be filled by enmity, or by someone else. Bitterness, hatefulness, sarcasm, caustic criticism, or horrible silence may occupy the void created by the absence of friendly conversation, touching, sharing, and togetherness.

Although I loved Bill and Jan, and was concerned for them, I did not want to sit there and absorb thirty years of garbage into my mind and spirit when it was obviously a conversation they had had before without results. I didn't need to hear them bringing up their old life again, but they did need help.

They had been believers in Christ for only four years and their lives had already been dramatically changed. Now they needed to apply that salvation to this area of their lives, but only the Lord could do it. God wanted to change their married life, just as He had changed their individual lives, and He would do it.

Jesus is the "Counsellor."[1] Any counsel given must come from Him, and His Word. Otherwise, it is simply good advice. *The difference between good news and good advice can be the difference between life and death.*

Many is the man who stands behind the pulpit on a Sunday morning and delivers good advice instead of the good news of the Gospel. Thousands die spiritually as a result.

That night I was fully aware that it was the blood of Jesus that had saved Bill and Jan, not my own, and that Jesus' blood was sufficient to complete the work in them that God had begun. When I was assured of the willingness of their hearts to obey whatever God would tell them, the

Holy Spirit was released in me to speak the "word" God wanted them to hear.

"Why don't you circumcise your marriage?" I startled them by asking.

"What?" They looked at each other with astonishment and then turned to me and said, "We've never heard of such a thing."

"Well, I really haven't either until just now," I said. At least I had not heard it put quite that way.

Years before, while pastoring in Northern California, I was led of the Lord into an intense ten days of purification of my life. It was a time when the Lord impressed me to leave everything I was doing, get in my car, and without any money or means of support, depend on Him totally for everything I was to need — gas, food, lodging, a place to go.

On the eighth day of those ten "days of purification," I went back home, asked my wife to continue with me, and we drove to a hotel near the beach. There the next day in prayer, I read in the book of Joshua where the children of Israel were circumcised "the second time."[2] The first time was before they left Egypt. Now, after they had entered Canaan with a new generation born after leaving Egypt, God required it again of the men, and of the nation.

I understood that circumcision represented two basic things: the putting away of the unclean, and the establishment of a covenant relationship.

My understanding when reading that scripture that day was that the Lord wanted to put away the things that were hurtful in the relationship I had with my wife. I also understood that He meant for the two of us to enter into a renewal of our marriage covenant by repenting of the past, allowing God by His Spirit to melt our hearts together in love, and to start afresh, building upon all the positive and blessed aspects of our new relationship.

When Nancy and I knelt across the bed from each other that night, and prayed together with our earnest and intense desire to please God, it was as though time stood still. God forgave me of all the negative thoughts, words, motives, and deeds, gave me a new appreciation, affection, desire and love for my wife that was so pure and precious — it can only be described as God's putting within me *agape* love, His own love, for my wife.

It was at that moment that all the hurts, pains, sorrows and suffering were wiped away from both of us and a renewal of the marriage covenant took place in our spirits. From then until now I have loved my wife with a love that I never knew was possible.

Without my realizing it, the Spirit of God had brought that reference to the circumcised marriage to my lips with Bill and Jan that night. I had never directly ministered to anyone before what God had ministered to Nancy and me that day, but now I could see that God wanted Bill and Jan to have that circumcised marriage also.

"Look," I began, "rather than going back and digging up all that buried garbage with all its putridness and stench, why not ask God to circumcise your marriage? Put away the uncleanness of the past thirty years and renew your marriage with a covenant in God that will rejuvenate it.

"God can do more by His Spirit in ten seconds than we can do in ten lifetimes. It's what Christ came for. The New Birth is for the totality of our lives, not just a 'soulish' experience.

"You've got to be willing to bury the past, not resurrect it. God can circumcise your hearts in marriage just as He did with sin in your hearts when you were converted. Old things can pass away and all things become new in your marriage, just as occurred in salvation. God can do what no man can do.

"If you're willing, I mean really willing, to ask God to work a miracle in your lives, then the Lord is ready to perform it. It's up to you."

Bill and Jan sat silent for a minute under the impact of what they had just heard. Slowly they turned to gaze at each other, searching for an answer they both hoped for but weren't sure they would find. Moments later, satisfied with what they saw in each other's eyes, they turned to me and Bill spoke for both of them.

"Let's do it," he said.

"Follow me in prayer," I said, and they bowed their heads.

They followed me in prayer, repeating the words that I used, and confessed their errors, mistakes and sins. They admitted their hates, angers, jealousies, and asked God to forgive them of the hurts they had inflicted on each other and themselves. Both of them spoke aloud their desire to put away the past, with all its uncleanness. They asked God to circumcise their hearts, they confessed their love for each other, they renewed their marriage vows of covenant while still in prayer, and they thanked God for what He was doing in their lives.

At the finish of the prayer, the presence of the Lord was so real in that hotel room, His power was so great, that we all sat in total silence before the awesomeness of God.

Slowly Jan relaxed, melted, into the arms of her husband. Bill caressed her arm and put his cheek on the top of her head. She sighed and whispered, "Wow." It was such a solemn, holy, sacred moment for them.

Several minutes later, while still cuddled against his chest, Jan opened her eyes, looked at me mistily, and then said so softly that I could hardly hear her, "I'd hate to tell you what I'm thinking right now."

"Probably about a room in this hotel," I said.

She smiled. Then the two of them straightened up to leave, but he did not let go of her. A man who had just admitted to me that he had a hard time being tender or wanting to touch, a man who had seldom caressed his wife in thirty years, now could not let go of her.

"I have prayed for this for four years, since I got saved and was able to pray," he said, "but I really never thought it would happen."

Bill and Jan found what was missing. He found his manhood, and she found her femininity. Together they found a new marriage.

Leaving arm in arm, they were a joyous couple, free in mind and spirit, enjoying a circumcised marriage.

God is not a magician, but He does work miracles.

A few weeks later I called Bill and Jan to see how they were doing. I wanted to relate their experience to a group of men I would be speaking to, but I wanted to be sure of the results first.

"How's it going, Bill?"

"We're on our honeymoon," he said. "We've learned to communicate. We've fallen in love."

"Physically, too? She's more than a best friend now?"

"Unbelievable. We've begun to practice the principles of intercession, too. It is so true that prayer produces intimacy. The intimate times we have together now are just, just..."

"Heavenly," I finished for him. He had answered my question. Later in a meeting, he and Jan stood and testified to the entire crowd what God had done for them.

God does circumcise the hearts of those who ask for it and are willing. God is faithful to His Word.

PART III:
MONEY

14
MASTER OR SERVANT

Sex and money are both expressions of love.

"It is more blessed to give than to receive,"[1] is the principle of the Kingdom taught in God's Word. That is true of both sex and money. The blessing is in the giving, not the getting.

How important is money?

Our Lord Jesus Christ was betrayed because of the "love of money." Ananias and Sapphira lied about their money through their fear of failure — theirs, the Church's, or Christ's. In his hatred of the Gospel, Demetrius caused a rebellion against the Apostle Paul because of the loss of his revenue derived from the worship of the goddess Diana. Paul's ship was wrecked because of the greed of its owners, and only Paul's intercession saved the crew from death. Jezebel hated Elijah and tried to kill him because of the loss of revenue which came about through the destruction of her prophets and their ministries.

Money, money, money.

It's life's "support system." For money men will sell their souls, women their bodies, and everyone is tempted to lose their virtue.

Men spend the majority of their time on earth thinking about money.

In divorce, money and children are the greatest causes of litigation.

Governments fall when corrupted by money's misuse.

People perish from its lack, unable to buy food.

Families are destroyed from the stress both of having too much of it, and not having enough of it. The "haves" and "have nots" still divide the world — and homes.

Men worship what money can do.

Men worry with it, and without it.

Worry is a substitute for prayer.

When our Lord said, "Seek ye first the kingdom of God...,"[2] He knew why He said it. It was and is because "...all these things shall be added unto you" when your faith is placed primarily and fundamentally in God as life's priority.

"Ye cannot serve God and mammon,"[3] is a principle of life. God comes first. Faith in God first makes faith for everything else possible. God knows what is best for us, and "...no good thing will he withhold from them that walk uprightly."[4]

Dave wanted to be a success. College, business, everything was keyed to succeeding in this world. His idea of success was to "be somebody." To do that, he needed to prosper financially. To achieve that goal, he had to climb the corporate ladder.

However, every promotion he set his heart upon he missed. Somehow, all the things he sought simply seemed to elude his grasp. There was constant emotional turmoil in him, and his home. When things went well on the job, he was fine. When they did not go well, he was in distress — and that distress was communicated to his wife and family. Their life was a "roller coaster," a "yo-yo," up and down from day to day.

His wife and children, who loved him deeply and dearly, bore the brunt of his emotional outbursts, impatience and intemperateness due to his frustrations. The people he was upset with on the job never heard about it — but those at home who loved him, cared for him, and prayed for him, suffered the effects of his hostilities toward others.

Dave's life was ruled by circumstances, not faith.

Dave gauged his success by corporate achievement, while God gauges it by character development. Christlikeness is the epitome of character development.

Dave never obtained what he sought, because he put "things" first — and expected God to be added to them.

Carl was different.

While Dave thought his problem was people — Carl thought his problems were overdue bills, lack of money, bad fortune, and a wife who could never make their money go far enough. His depression was unknown to both him and his wife, but it was there, and was a constant drain on the entire family. It sapped the very vitality out of their home life.

Carl's problem wasn't money. It was greed, willfulness, laziness, and an obdurate spirit. He wanted what he wanted when he wanted it, and when he couldn't pay for it, it was always the fault of something or someone other than himself.

Issues of the flesh come from issues of the spirit.

Carl dealt with a "slack hand." Poverty is promised to those who deal that way. It is as certain as the sun, moon and stars. A "slack hand" is the same as laziness.

Both Dave and Carl put God second in their lives. God was not their primary source of life, nor the solution to their problems. God was a convenience to them. Worship was something to be engaged in only when it was convenient to their schedule or feelings.

God is never a convenience in life.

God must be sought after to be found.

His wisdom must be sought after as one would seek for buried treasure.

It is God Who gives wisdom to get wealth.

Jesus once said that it was as hard for a rich man to enter the Kingdom of Heaven as it was for a camel to go through the eye of a needle. What He was referring to was men's dependence on money instead of God — their failure to recognize the Lord as the source of their wealth.

A wise man looks to God as his source.

Though God seeks for man, and has since Eden when He called to Adam, "Where art thou?"[5] it is not until a man is willing to seek God first with his whole heart that God will be found by him.

God is not lost. Man is.

God cannot discover Himself to men until men are willing to discover themselves to Him.

God must be the source of all, or else He is the solution to nothing.

God never settles for second place.

Slavery hasn't left us, it has just changed complexion. It is green and silver, the color of money. Money can be the master or the servant, make a man a slave or be a servant to him.

Esau, in the Bible, is called a "profane person"[6] because he sold his birthright for a mess of pottage. He treated his God-given gift with contempt by trading it for a moment's pleasure. He debased that which was holy simply to feed his flesh.

Balaam "prostituted" his God-given gift. He bartered with the enemy of God's people, and to this day is known as a traitor to righteousness. He is listed in God's roll call of infamy.

Balaam prophesied correctly, but privately advised Balak to cause Israel to eat things sacrificed to idols and to tempt Israel to commit fornication.

Balaam used for gold what God had given for glory. He profaned the gift of his God, just as Esau did. He traded his gift for pleasure.

Money itself is amoral. The morality of money is given to it by the nature of the man with it. Money can be a blessing or cursing, depending on its use. Man determines the meaning of money.

"The love of money is the root of all evil,"[7] is the Word of the Lord.

The lust of money makes slaves of men.

The proper use of money is to produce prosperity.

Wise investments lead to financial security and stability.

A man has a tendency to see the worth of his manhood in terms of money.

But men were meant to fulfill their sense of manhood through a relationship with God, not through material gain.

However, God never meant for men to live without gain. He meant for them to seek the Kingdom of God first, then gain would be added to them.

Prosperity is the natural, sequentially ordered result of righteousness in the life. Wherever there is righteousness, there is prosperity. It is a principle of life.

That's true whether in money or marriage. A right relationship produces prosperity.

"Blessed is the man....(whose) delight is in the law of the Lord....Whatever he does prospers"[8] is how the psalmist said it.

Poverty is an enemy. It is a blessing only to those who embrace it; a curse to those who don't.

Being poor and living in poverty are not necessarily the same. A "poverty syndrome" afflicts the poor and the rich alike, and can produce an aversion to financial health.

119

Ralph had a contract on his desk that was the largest he had ever been offered. He was a painting contractor and was successful in a small way, but he knew if he signed the contract it would necessitate hiring new help, buying new equipment, and being forced to expand his business.

While trying to make up his mind as to what he should do, he heard God's Word one Sunday morning: "To him that knoweth to do good, and doeth it not, to him it is sin."[9] He knew the word was for him.

If he knew to prosper and did not do it, it was sin. To refuse God's favor was to deny His prosperity.

Ralph realized that when God gave him an opportunity to enlarge his business, expand his influence, enable more money to flow into the work of the Lord — that not to do it would be the sin of unbelief. He saw that if he did not prosper when God wanted him to he would be sinning against God.

When God wanted Israel out of Egypt, it was to bring them into Canaan. God wanted Israel where He could show them His favor, and prosper them in all they did.

His promise was to prosper them. When they enjoyed their prosperity, God warned them not to think they had gained it all by their own hands or efforts, when it was His favor that gave them the wisdom and strength to get wealth.

Refusal to prosper is one aspect of the "poverty syndrome."

A man's rejection of God's desire to make his life better in every way through Jesus Christ is unfair — unfair to God's grace, to his family, his church, and community.

Men who fail to prosper through a sense of their own unworthiness have never understood that if they are in Christ, and Christ is in them, then their identity with the worthiness of Christ makes them worthy.

Jesus Christ is worthy of everything in heaven and on earth. Identification with Him gives worthiness to a man's life. Everything we have from God is by faith in Christ, and in His worthiness.

Jesus makes worthy the worst of us.

My family and I learned this lesson the hard way. None of us will ever forget it.

When I went to buy a new car, I felt impressed to purchase a very comfortable car that my family could be content and satisfied with. However, I decided against it because I didn't consider myself worthy to have such a nice car.

I disobeyed God. He wanted me to prosper and I considered myself unworthy of His goodness.

The small car I finally bought instead became a "curse" to our family. It broke down constantly, was in the repair shop more than on the road, every member of the family had a wreck in it, the engine was replaced, also the transmission, and most of the body of the car.

Finally, after three years of torment, and after all the payments were made, I was sitting in a coffee shop when I saw a man who used to work at the dealership where I took my car for service. By that time I knew everyone there and they knew me. The man greeted me and asked if I still owned the "lemon." We laughed and I told him it was parked right out front.

He then asked if I wanted to sell it because the new car agency he was working for needed a "loaner," and they could use that car. I gave him the keys, told him to mail me a check with the transfer of ownership papers, called my daughter to come get me, and she and I rejoiced at the top of our lungs all the way home.

I was free.

My family had been victimized by my "poverty attitude." I had confused "humility" with disobedience. I would never make that mistake again.

For so long our churches taught against the evils of riches that in the minds of believers poverty almost became synonymous with godliness. That attitude permeated every area of our lives so that the blessings of God in this life were not even sought nor appreciated by the very ones for whom God paid the ultimate price to provide them.

The result was that God's own children did not have even the necessities of life, much less the funds to preach the Gospel in all the world.

It is not wrong to be rich; it is only wrong to trust in riches, to think you have the power to get them apart from God's favor, to use them only for self, to lust after them, seek them through "get-rich-quick" schemes, desire them immorally, or to obtain or use them illegally.

Riches are not wrong. It is what they do to us that is wrong. Riches with righteousness can be a blessing.

The deceitfulness of riches is the fact that when you think you have enough, it never is, and you need still more. There is never any contentment.

Contentment is necessary because it eliminates monetary deception.

Vertigo is a common problem of deceitfulness to those who fly airplanes. Vertigo is deception in direction. When flying in clouds, or in dense fog, without instruments, it is common for pilots to think they are flying straight on course while heading straight for the ground.

There is a spiritual and financial vertigo that occurs in people's lives. Thinking they are upward bound, they are actually spiraling head first toward a catastrophe.

Harold was a business genius. Everything he touched in his business prospered. When more money was needed, he instituted a "development program" through which people could invest in his business. Although there was a limit established by government authorities as to how much could be received from such a program, when that limit was reached, Harold did not stop soliciting or receiving funds in obedience to the law, but continued contrary to it.

He was deceived into thinking that he could disobey the law and still maintain the business. He was wrong. Eventually he was forced out of his business, it was taken over by others, and Harold never recovered. He died ignominiously instead of gloriously.

Financial vertigo.

Phil's problems differed. He was deceived by his own greed. While guiding a thriving national business, he was contacted by a very mysterious person who promised him a fortune. Believing the promise was real, and refusing friends' counsel to be careful, Phil began to plan, purchase, and "invest" the riches he was assured were coming, but which were not yet his. Instead of continuing with the fiscal responsibility that had made him successful in the past, he succumbed to a "get-rich-quick" fraud and in the end he lost everything.

The pattern for failure is: Deception — Distraction — Dislocation — Destruction.

When money is not loved, but is only used for purposes that are good, right and holy, then money can be good, right and holy. This is why monetary offerings made to the Lord can be consecrated as holy to Him.

The pattern for increase is: Identification — Involvement — Investment — Increase.

It's basic to life.

Department stores use this pattern to produce profits. They advertise to get you to identify with their products, then to enter the store to become involved with looking at the merchandise, then when you invest through a purchase, they gain the increase.

The same pattern applies at home.

When you identify with your son by going to his baseball game, and as a result you become involved in each other's lives, you actually make an investment in your relationship. The end result is an increase in family solidarity.

Successful salesmen are those who are identified with their company, involved in marketing the product, making an investment of time and energy in it, and as a result, have personal increase from it.

Don't be a slave.

Make money your servant.

Money is for serving.

Money is to be our servant, we are not to serve money.

Being a servant to money is a bondage to any man.

Be the master of your finances, not the servant.

15
GIVING AND RECEIVING

From the time Jim married, his wife handled the checkbook, paid the bills, and tried to balance the budget. When the checkbook would not balance anymore, she got a job in an effort to make up the difference. During the period of months after she went to work, they paid their bills, and even began a savings account. They were both thrilled.

But her motivation to work was partly from fear. When she spent even five dollars more than what he considered necessary for groceries, he found fault with her. His "humorous" gibe was, "You keep the books in line, and I'll keep you in line."

Then one bright and brilliant spring Saturday, Jim came home driving a new pickup, with a trailer behind it and a boat on the trailer. When his wife went out to see what he was so excited about, she asked whose it all was. "Ours," he proudly confessed.

She knew that his unilateral decision — made without consulting her — would throw their checkbook completely out of balance again. And she also knew whose fault it would be.

When Jim came home from work on Monday, he found a note informing him that his wife and children were gone, and would not return. He was furious. He blamed her for everything, never once thinking of the hurt that led to her decision to leave.

Jim was foolish. He said he had faith in God, but never acted as if he had faith in his wife. Love for God is evidenced by love for others. Faith in God is often exhibited by faith in others. Trusting God completely means to trust Him to take care of those around you.

Jim was foolish. At heart he was a very selfish person.

Nabal was a fool.

The Bible tells us that Nabal's flocks and herds were protected by David. But when David sent for an offering, Nabal was incensed, denied that he knew David, and angrily refused the request. Nabal's wife, Abigail, knew of David and what he had done to protect them and their possessions. So when she heard of her husband's refusal to send an offering, she prepared it herself and took it to David.

Hers was a righteous act, done in faith, with great gratitude.

When Nabal learned what had been done, his heart turned to stone and days later he died. David married Abigail.

The "Nabals" of this world are men who refuse to tithe, claiming they don't know God, that what they have has come because of their own efforts and not because of anything God has done for them. Women married to such men — who must make up the family tithe from whatever money they have because of their husband's selfish, self-centered attitude toward God — are the "Abigails" of this world.

Unlike Nabal, these men have not lied, but their cars, their jobs and businesses have. Sickness has caused doctors' bills that have devoured their savings, and during all of their distresses, they have gone right on rejecting the truth that it is their arrogant and unbelieving attitude that has caused all their problems.

Tithing is necessary, whether you believe it or not, because it is only for those who tithe that God promises to rebuke the devourer.

Men cannot outgive God. God will be debtor to no man. Giving to God without His giving more in return would essentially make God a debtor to the giver. That can't be done. Of course, God doesn't always give back the way men do.

When you are tithing and obeying Him, God will give health so doctors' bills don't devour your income. He will give you favor in buying a car so that it is not a "lemon" and devour your income on repairs, or keep you constantly in debt — so your debts devour you.

God will enable you to come through difficult times in marriage so there is no divorce, and no alimony or child support to devour your income.

Don't laugh! I have listened to men complain about these very things, never acknowledging that their refusal to put God first in their lives is the very cause of their ills.

Others have thanked God for His bountiful blessings, and their delight in the Lord is revealed in their generosity toward His ministry.

Tithing a portion to God from what He has provided for you is basic to financial health.

Tithing is an open, visible, external evidence of dependence on, and faith in, God. In the school of faith, tithing is the first grade.

Faith in God has two visible, physical evidences. One is the healing of the body, and the other is the use of money.

We know that Jesus went often to the temple to worship, and, while there, would oftentimes sit over against the treasury and watch how people cast in their money. It was there that He commended a widow who threw in only two mites, saying she had given more than all the others because she had cast in ''all that she had.''[1]

You can tell a man's character better by his use of money than by his way of worship.

Zacchaeus showed his faith by his willingness to take the riches he had garnered through illegal and immoral means and give them back to God by giving to the poor. Scripture tells us that giving to the poor is the same as lending to the Lord. The physical evidence of the internal work of faith in the life of Zacchaeus was shown by the use of his money.

Ananias and Sapphira were reserving something for themselves in case of failure. Their unbelief and lack of faith was shown in their use of money. Moral cowardice was their undoing.

Moral cowardice caters to the carnal at the expense of the holy.

Moral cowardice is a bane to manhood.

Covetousness is a curse to manhood.

Being Christlike in your manhood requires a generous spirit. Generosity enlarges the spirit. Covetousness closes the spirit. Covetousness is a form of idolatry, because it is the worship of self. In Proverbs we read, ''The liberal soul shall be made fat: and he that watereth shall be watered also himself.''[2]

Giving and receiving requires wisdom and strategy.

At one time Hank was extremely successful in business, but then for ten years he struggled. As a real estate broker, he had experienced the favor of God upon his life and financially prospered above many of his peers.

Then he made a mistake that was to cost him dearly. Because of lack of wisdom, he made an error in the God-given strategy he had been following. Hank was to learn what the scripture means when it says, ''For if you wander beyond the teaching of Christ, you will leave God behind.''[3]

Believing that God wanted him to prosper, he had begun to practice "seed-faith" giving. Each financial increase enabled him to give even more "seed" from which to reap his financial harvest.

Enjoying the benefits of the blessings, he began to travel, enjoy some very pleasurable outings, and entertain his friends. He was generous with God, and he was generous with others, giving both time and money.

But, in his belief that all he had to do was exercise "seed-faith" to find financial favor with God, Hank began to allow his work habits to suffer. He skipped days at the office, did not make his sales calls when he should, no longer felt the need to "pound the pavement," knock on doors, or to make an effort to meet people where they were.

Eventually his attitude and actions began to take their toll. Business fell off, and soon his income was failing. Hank couldn't understand it. He was still giving, still believing, but the money wasn't coming in.

He was guilty of dealing "with a slack hand."[4]

He had taken the truth of God's Word, carried it too far, and fell into error.

Error oftentimes is nothing but truth carried to the extreme.

Magical thinking was Hank's problem. He forgot to work.

"A lazy man is brother to the saboteur,"[5] is what Proverbs says.

Hank sabotaged himself, but he learned his lesson and is now working as he did before. He is still sowing his "seed-gifts," but he won't make that mistake of dealing "with a slack hand" again. He's another grade higher in the school of faith.

God always gives a strategy for victory.

God's wisdom is the strategy. His glory is in the victory. Men pray for victory, and God gives a strategy.

Moses, Gideon, David, Elijah — all achieved great victories in their lives because God gave them the strategy necessary to obtain it.

God's strategy for Gideon was not simply the use of pitchers and lanterns; it first involved total agreement and unity among the troops under his command. That's why He reduced the size of his armed force. God knew that Gideon's army would be stronger with 300 men all doing the same thing, than with 30,000 all doing things differently.

"Can two walk together, except they be agreed?"[6] is not just a prophetic pronouncement nor a principle for marriage encounters, but it is also a principle of the Kingdom that is applicable in the totality of life.

The Bible says that when Israel came up out of Egypt, they came "harnessed."[7] They were all in unity. Agreement is part of God's strategy. In fact, it is basic to all successful strategy, whether divine or carnal.

Agreement is basic in successful marriages and businesses. It is basic in managing money and raising children. Agreement will always be part of the strategy God gives you.

God's promises are conditional; His love is unconditional.

God loves us whether we meet His conditions or not. However, if we do not meet His conditions through faith, we cannot obtain His promises. Whether we are rich or poor, have or have not, has nothing to do with God's love, but with our faith.

God gave King David the promise of the throne in Israel, but David had to fight to obtain the fulfillment of the promise. There was a strategy given, a fight fought, and a victory won. David ascended to the throne.

To expect victory without being willing to fight is foolishness.

The struggle for your financial health may lead to problems and difficulties, reverses and hardships, but God will give the wisdom and the strategy to win over all your enemies as you seek Him and obey Him.

Ask God for your own strategy for financial health. Discover a place of agreement instead of making selfish, unilateral decisions. Start giving of yourself and let your spirit be enlarged.

God is generous.

God lavishes His grace on sinners.

He gives great glory to His saints.

His forgiveness is as boundless as His love.

Great grace is given to His Church.

"...it is your Father's good pleasure to give you the kingdom."[8] You don't have to convince God to give you what He has already said is His good pleasure to give.

Be God-like. Be generous. Be holy.

Be generous in spirit. Be forgiving.

Be generous with God, with your family, with others.

16
DEBT OF LOVE

There is an old saying that "we get too soon old and too late smart."

Wisdom is the principal need in our life. The Bible teaches that, along with it, we are to get understanding. Wisdom is the right use of knowledge. Understanding is just applied, anointed common sense.

Wisdom gives long good life, riches, honor, pleasure and peace. Wisdom provides for every need in a man's life. Wisdom, not money, is man's basic need. You can have money, but to be without wisdom to use it is to be in constant need — never able to come to the place of financial stability.

The lack of knowledge in the right use of money has killed more than one marriage, and there are thousands crippled from it even now.

Bad communication and bad sex which derive from bad financial habits make for a bad marriage.

A man who sees things that he desires, and has a lust for them, develops a love for the money that can be used to acquire them. He is guilty of the sin of the "lust of the eyes."[1] Men lust for things, and as a result lust for, or love, money.

There are really only three basic sins known to man. They are: the lust of the flesh, the lust of the eyes, and the pride of life. When Jesus went to the "mount of temptation" and was tempted by the devil for forty days, He was tested in these three areas.

First, the devil offered Jesus a piece of bread, which is the temptation of the lust of the flesh. Then Satan told Jesus to prove that He was the Son of God by casting Himself down from the pinnacle of the temple and having the angels bear Him up. This was the temptation of the pride of life. Finally, the devil told Jesus that he would give Him all the kingdoms of the world if only He would bow down and worship him. This was the temptation of the lust of the eyes. Jesus withstood all three of these tests.

After Jesus had overcome these temptations, He came down off the mountain and was launched into His ministry.

All the temptations men face today are a result of one of these three basic sins. And much of the problem men have with money stems from the lust of the eyes, a desire to possess.

Every man will be tested in all three areas, and there is no exception. The example of our own Lord is the proof.

Just as the pornography addict is captive to his lusts, so the moneymonger becomes the slave to his greed. It is not just the miser, the one who hoards money, who is held captive by it, but also the spendthrift who wastes it.

Men who place themselves so heavily in debt that they cannot take a day off, enjoy life, or meet the needs of their family are the servants of money. They are never free to live as they desire because they are slaves to their debt. Instead of getting out of debt through a God-given strategy, they get impatient and caught up with the lust of the eyes in wanting some new thing, and run up the bills again.

Unlike God, there are men who delight to put you in debt. Usury is a sin, and lending institutions that encourage borrowing at ultra-high interest rates are engaging in it. Our government tries to control usury, but they cannot control human greed.

Bankers and others who make their living from the interest paid on money by those in debt are always thinking of ways to increase debt. Stress from debt payments afflicts entire nations.

Brazil, so heavily in debt, declared a moratorium on interest payments to the banks which had loaned the money. On the verge of bankruptcy, just from the interest payments on its notes, an entire nation suffers.

The banks that encouraged the unpayable debt are now incurring heavy losses, and may themselves be bankrupt — which in turn could trigger a chain reaction of financial devastation worldwide.

Stress for the individual man too heavily in debt from borrowing translates into every other area of life. It affects and afflicts everyone.

To men who are paying too high a price in the strain on their minds, bodies, marriages, families, and friends because of the debt load — God has a word of instruction:

"Owe no man any thing, but...love..."[2]

Get out of debt.

We live in a "credit card" society. Spend now, pay later. Instant gratification is the rule of the day.

God does not want His men enslaved by unpaid debts, and so wrapped up with tomorrows that they are irresponsive to the Word of the Lord in their todays. They live their lives to pay their debts.

Your life is worth too much to spend it for debt payments. You were born free, and God wants you to live free, a debtor to no man of anything but love.

It is impossible truly to love a person you inwardly resent because you owe him money.

Quit using credit cards for purchases when you know there will be no money to pay for them.

Worry is borrowing against tomorrow.

So is debt.

Pay your bills when they come due. When payments cannot be made, communicate that fact to those you owe. Failure to communicate creates fear — and fear will always cause a negative reaction. Avoid the negative by taking a positive action. Communicate. Overcoming *your* fear will overcome theirs.

To live contentedly and happily — live within your means. God has promised to provide food, clothing and shelter to those who love and serve Him. Beyond that, it is a matter of individual desire and faith as to what you will have. If you are content with just these three bare essentials, that's fine, live that way. But if you desire more, more can be created from your desires.

"Godliness with contentment is great gain"[3] is not just a statement in the Bible, but a basic principle of life. Discontentment in life is generally caused by lust. Lust is never satisfied; love is easily satisfied. Lust is insatiable. So is hell. Men who love what they are doing are easily satisfied.

"If you love Me, keep My commandments,"[4] is what Jesus told us. Obedience is the evidence of love. Too often disobedience is caused by lack of knowledge. We perish from lack of knowledge.

Obedience is God's only method of protection for our lives.

Disobedience puts us outside God's protective custody.

When you obey God, you trust Him for tomorrow.

Our tomorrows are taken care of by today's obedience.

One man told me that he had solved his debt crisis and been freed from the bondage of money by performing "plastic surgery" on his wife — he cut off all her credit cards!

Financial health does not depend on how much you make, but on how much you save. And how much you save depends on how much you spend.

This is why you and your wife must be in agreement. Once you two have agreed on getting out of debt, or becoming tithers, or having victory over your financial crisis, or being better stewards, then you release the power of God to work in your lives. A man who tries to do this unilaterally is going to have a difficult time. If his wife absolutely will not come into a place of agreement, he needs to take that situation to the Lord until she does.

Budgets are good only if a man abides by them. A budget not kept is no budget at all.

God is a God of "specificity."

Be specific in all you do.

Inadequate records make for inadequate communication. Poor records are unreliable messengers.

Be wise.

Live within your means.

Keep adequate records.

Get out of debt.

Owe love and nothing more.

As a practical reminder of the principles of handling money, refer often to the list below.

1. God is your Source.
2. Seek God first in everything.
3. Decisions require responsibility.
   Decisions cannot be unilateral in marriage.
4. Tithing is basic visible evidence of faith.
5. Get out of debt.

6. Start where you are with what you have.
7. Live within your means.
8. To obey God today is to trust Him for tomorrow.
9. Keep adequate records.
10. Be generous with God — and with others.

17
THE PRINCIPLES OF INVESTING

"Use it or lose it."

That isn't exactly the way the Lord Jesus Christ said it in teaching His investment principles in the "Parable of the Pounds," but it is the essence of the "Law of Increase and Decline," which He taught in the parable.

Jesus taught about a man who, before leaving on a trip, gave his servants each a pound. When he returned, the first servant had invested and made a ten-fold increase, the second had made a five-fold increase, but the third had hidden the one pound he had received. The first and second servants were commended by their master, but he scolded the third servant for being too timid even to place his pound in a bank where he may have earned some interest on it.

The principle is: By use you possess and gain; by disuse you decline and lose.

A man with an eighteen-inch bicep who is able to lift a one-hundred-pound barbell single-handed, would be foolish to put his arm in a sling and not use it for fear of hurting it through exercise. To keep his strength, he must exercise his muscles. By doing so, he will not only keep what he has, but increase it.

To gain energy, you must give energy.

Only a fool thinks the way to retain or gain energy is by resting continually to conserve what he has. An enervation will take place through rest, while the man constantly putting himself to the test by exercising will become more and more energetic.

The principle of the parable is that hoarding causes loss, while investing will not only allow you to keep what you have, but gain more through the use of it.

The proper use of money, is to prosper by its use. It's the same with time and talent.

The business world says it this way, "It takes money to make money."

In desiring to invest, save, or own a business, many people want to start "big," "at the top," not realizing that giant oak trees come from small acorns. "Despise not the day of small beginnings" is a biblical principle.

You cannot invest thousands before investing just one, or make millions of dollars until you have made the first dollar. It's the first one that counts, all others will follow. Investing and forgiving both have the same principle — start where you are with what you have.

Every man wants to invest something that will cause him to gain from it. There are three things a man can invest: time, talent and treasure. When you think of investments, do not limit your thinking to the investments of your money in stocks, real estate, or a new business. Every day of your life you invest twenty-four God-given hours in something, or some things. Every time you use your talent, either as an accountant, a trained soldier, a pilot, or any other occupation, you are investing that talent.

Here are some guidelines for investing:

1. You invest in people.

A company is only as good as the personnel who manage or control it.

My son, Paul, called me one day asking advice concerning an investment he was contemplating making. He informed me that some very important people were investors in the company. He named some of the musical artists, pastors, influential businessmen, and others who were investing in the enterprise.

"Who owns the company, who is the president, and who is going to run it?" I asked him.

"I don't know. Why?" he asked.

"You don't invest in investors, you invest in the corporate officers," I explained. "A company, business, government, or ministry is only as good as the character of the men controlling it."

Paul did not know who the officers of the corporation were, or who they had chosen as the Chief Executive Officer, so my advice to him was to keep his money.

The newspaper this very day carried the story of a company founded by a minister who is alleged to have lost $12,000,000 of the investors' money. Many of these people had based their decision to invest in the company on the names of the other investors. One man was desolate because he had lost $250,000, his entire life's savings.

Tragic, but so common.

Con-artists obtain their reputation vicariously through association with men of good character. They use people to influence people. Devoid of integrity themselves, they cover their chicanery with the aura of honesty derived from acquaintance with men of real worth.

Just because a man calls himself a "brother," does not mean that he has the character or ability you want to invest in. "You are not to keep company with anyone who claims to be a brother Christian but...is a swindler.... Don't even eat lunch with such a person,"[1] is the scriptural injunction. Avoid such a person; he has a rapacious character.

A swindler in church is still a swindler. Saintly sinners are still sinners.

When you invest, remember you are investing in the character of the company, which is derived from the character of the men managing it.

2. Before investing, investigate.

Integrity is the essence of character — faithfulness is the cornerstone.

"Only a simpleton believes what he is told! A prudent man checks to see where he is going,"[2] is what the proverb says.

Your peace of mind and heart is the best evidence that what you are doing is right. Peace is the umpire for doing the will of God.[3]

Integrity is needed by both parties in an investment.

Wallace sold everything he had, to buy an interest in an automobile firm with a man he had come to know through association in church activities. Six years later, Wallace left town after having lost everything. He came to see me after he had moved away to escape from the place of his tragedy and trauma.

We sat on the jetty overlooking the harbor near where I live, and he told me what had happened. When he finished, I asked him when it was that he knew he was in trouble and would lose it all.

"I realized it when we made the deal," he said. "At the very moment we shook hands in the living room of my home, I knew it was wrong."

"Why under God's heaven did you go through with it?" I asked.

"Because I didn't want to face the fact that it was wrong. I was too embarrassed to admit that I had made a mistake," he confessed to me.

"You mean, Wally, that you went ahead and lost everything just because of your pride?"

He nodded. He hadn't been honest with himself. He hadn't finished his investigation by looking into his own spirit to see if there was peace there.

An internal witness is always better than an external circumstance.

Fortuitous circumstance can be blown away with any passing wind, but the peace the Lord gives is an anchor to the soul.

Investigate, then let the peace of God be your umpire for doing His will in your life.

3. Risk, don't gamble.

Everything in life has risk. You must take risks in whatever venture you undertake and every time you make a decision. But risk is different from gambling. Gambling is risking on chance.

"Wealth from gambling quickly disappears; wealth from hard work grows,"[4] says Proverbs.

One world-famous gambler wrote in his autobiography why he believes he is successful while most other gamblers die penniless: "When I'm hot, I'm hot," he wrote. "When I'm not, I quit!"

There is a season to everything under the sun. There is seedtime and harvest, and the season can't be changed. Seedtime never follows harvest, any more than spring follows summer.

There are seasons in life also. Seasons to sow, seasons to reap. Only a fool will try to harvest in springtime. Knowing the seasons in life — when the time has come to sow by investing, or to wait — is vital to being able to reap the increase.

God's Word tells us to "be instant in season, out of season...."[5] meaning that constancy is one of the virtues of manhood.

143

Our constancy in our relationship with the Lord will cause us to recognize our seasons of sowing, waiting, or reaping, and keep us from regarding a gamble as a risk.

A wise man respects the seasons of his life and refuses to invest when "out of season" on a gamble.

4. It must be in writing.

Misunderstanding is the tool of strife. Friends can become enemies through misunderstanding. That is why in our ministry offices we have a saying, "If it isn't in writing, it doesn't exist."

People miss God's best through impatience, and lose God's best through misunderstanding.

Trust is the basis of friendship, but a poor memory undermines trust.

The way the Bible teaches it is that "reliable communication permits progress."[6]

That is why you don't ever invest in anything that is not spelled out on paper and signed — a reliable communication.

William and Lawrence are friends of mine who have been best friends with each other for over thirty-five years. For all their years of friendship, they have been business partners. Both of them are men of integrity and true Christian character. The remarkable thing about them is that in all those years, they have never had a misunderstanding.

In all their dealings, both personally and financially, they have had their agreements put in writing. Unless it was in writing, they never ventured into any investment, purchase, or sale.

Even when they borrowed money personally from their own company, they each agreed to it, then signed the terms of their agreement. Whenever there was a question about any transaction or agreement, it was a simple matter to refer to the contract made, and the difference in opinion was reconciled and the matter was settled. Their written agreements never detracted from their trust in each other as friends, but allowed them to transcend poor memories and misunderstandings to have a harmonious relationship through the years.

God's Kingdom rests on covenants, Satan's kingdom thrives on misunderstandings. Leaving room for misunderstanding is leaving room for the devil.

Understanding — like agreement — produces power; misunderstanding — like disagreement — results in powerlessness.

God put His Word and His agreement with us in writing. Learn to put yours in writing as well. Never leave room for misunderstanding. Write it down.

5. Don't live with death.

If you lose an investment, bury it.

Men who have failed and refuse to try again live with death.

Some years ago, my wife and I knew a lovely lady who lost her husband when he suffered a heart attack and died. She loved him so much, had been married to him so long, and grieved over him so deeply, that she left everything of his exactly the way it was the day he died, right down to the toiletries in the bathroom.

She was living with death.

As a result of living with death, she lost friends, her job, and her health. One morning while reading her Bible, she was struck by these words spoken by the Lord: "Moses my servant is dead; now therefore arise...."[7] She knew this was a word for her.

She gave away everything that had belonged to her husband, sold their house, and moved to another town. There she obtained a new job and made a whole new life for herself. Her health improved. She was alive. She made an investment in life and began to live again.

Learn to live. Bury your past failures, not the talents you still have.

Admit your loss. Learn from it. Then go on to better things. Don't carry past mistakes like a dead carcass.

The Apostle Paul wrote, "O wretched man that I am! who shall deliver me from the body of this death?"[8]

In Paul's day, the customary punishment for a person convicted of murder was to be chained to the body of the individual he had killed. Everywhere the guilty person went, he would drag with him the dead carcass of his victim. Eventually he would die from the weight of his burden.

Here, Paul was referring to his past life before he came to know Christ. He was crying for deliverance from the weight of his sins. When he received release from the Lord for his guilt, he wrote, "I thank God through Jesus Christ our Lord...."[9] Our answer for our past sins is the same.

Jesus came to give us life, and to give it more abundantly. You don't need to live with death.

6. Invest in producers.

In His "Parable of the Pounds," Jesus teaches another very important truth:

The man who does the least talks the most.

Doers don't waste time or cover their deeds with conversation.

Invest your time with men who inspire.
Invest your money with men who produce.
Invest your talent with men who create.

"Iron sharpens iron...."[10] is the biblical principle for surrounding yourself with those whose sharpness of mind and character will sharpen your own.

Don't be fooled by men who talk. Invest in men who produce.

7. Shadows are more fierce than reality.

When I was a young boy living in Los Angeles, my mother would sometimes ask me to go to the store in the evening after dark. I always walked in the middle of the street to avoid the shadows the trees made. The shadows looked fiercely dangerous. I avoided them at all cost.

As adults, the shadows are what we think others are thinking, and what we think others will do. We avoid confrontation for fear of what will happen. The shadows are always more fierce than reality.

You need the light from God's Word shed on your path to free you from the shadows. Don't avoid reality by being afraid of shadows.

Fear was the result of guilt in the life of Adam in the garden of Eden. That relationship still exists. "Perfect love casteth out fear..."[11] because perfect love has no guilt.

Men who borrow and don't repay suffer from guilt. Men who promise God and do not keep their commitment suffer guilt. Men avoid those toward whom they feel guilty, whether man or God.

Society is full of men who at one time were classified as "Christians," who still profess faith, but who have long since dropped all pretense of church attendance. The guilt from promises to God not kept ruptured their relationship both with God and the Church.

Guilt casts the biggest shadow.

Guilt is a killer.

When a person borrows money from you, your loan to him is an investment in him. If the debt remains unpaid, every time you see that man you will remember what is owed. He will be guilty of a failure to repay, but you will be the one who constantly thinks of it — and in so doing, you will be bearing his guilt. It will cast a shadow on your relationship.

The only way to be free from another person's guilt is to forgive him. The release through forgiveness frees you from his guilt. Why carry someone else's guilt in your life?

Forgive and live free. Get rid of the shadows. They are more fierce than reality. Seek God's view of what is happening because it is truth and reality.

8. Funds come from friends.

"Never abandon a friend — either yours or your father's. Then you won't need to go to a distant relative for help in your time of need"[12] the Bible says.

When in St. Louis, at a luncheon of businessmen, I was teaching this principle and told those in attendance that they should be concerned about making friends, not clients. An electrical contractor came to me afterward to express his appreciation for what was said.

"You know," he began, "I couldn't understand how my business has held up during this recession when others are having business problems. You just explained it to me. Today I have a number of contractors who just call me and tell me to come do their job, and they never ask me for a bid. Over the years we have become friends, and that is where my funds are coming from."

Repeat business comes from those who feel friendly.

An investment to make a friend will pay greater dividends than any company.

Jesus concluded the parable of the unjust steward with this principle.

"And I tell you, make friends for yourselves by means of unrighteous mammon [that is, deceitful riches, money, possessions], so that when it fails, they [those you have favored] may receive and welcome you into the everlasting habitations (dwellings)."[13]

This steward knew that if he could make enough friends before he was forced to leave his job, he would be able to make money again in a different position.

The host of a nationally syndicated television talk show was startled when I corrected him about how his financial dilemma was solved. He said the funds bailed him out, but I told him it was his friends who bailed him. He had made friends of his viewers so that, when difficulties arose, he was successful in his "friend-raising," not his "fund-raising."

Lack of friends causes lack of funds, and lack of funds can part the best of friends.

Making friends of clients and customers, by servicing them, will ensure that you have funds.

Servicing clients builds businesses.
Servicing congregations builds churches.
Servicing family members builds relationships.

9. Invest your life for your greatest good.

Any investment you make is always an investment of yourself.

Investing time is investing yourself.
Investing talent is investing yourself.
Investing your money is investing yourself.

In return for giving your life at your work, you receive money. What you do with your money reveals what you do with your life. Your money represents your life.

Where you invest your money shows where your life is invested.

Men without an investment in eternity don't tithe to the Lord or His Church. How much of a man's life is invested in the Kingdom of God is revealed by his investment in the offering plate. He who loves little, gives little. He who loves much, gives much.

The more time you give God, the more time you have for yourself. The more you give of yourself, the more you have to give.

Your life is in your giving.

That's true in marriage.

The more you give — the more you get.

You know how much Christ loves by how much He gave of Himself. He gave us His all. By His giving all, you know He is completely trustworthy. You can invest your whole life in Him and know the investment will reap dividends from now throughout eternity.

Invest in such a way that you will receive the increase in your relationship with your wife, children, church, job, and community. Don't invest in what will make someone else rich, or provide a good reputation for someone you don't know. Invest in what you know is good and right in your own life, in your own sphere of understanding.

The more you give, the more you get.

Investing your own life will always be your greatest investment.

Investing in the Kingdom of God is the wisest investment you will ever make.

10. Don't quit!

Never, never, never, never, never, never, never, never quit!

CONCLUSION

18

BUT THE GREATEST
OF THESE IS LOVE

"I love you."

Words are power, and these are the most powerful words in the human vocabulary. Nothing can compare with the power of these words spoken from the heart. They can change the fate of nations, or the destiny of man.

Love can make a king abdicate his throne, a pauper become a prince, a woman surrender her virtue, a boy do handstands, or a man work from sunup to sundown.

Nothing is as strong as love is.

Love is not a soft, tender little something that must be wrapped in tissue, laid on the shelf of the heart and only taken out occasionally to be admired.

Love works in overalls, jeans, cut-offs, and silk hats. It walks in boots, sandals, Johnston-Murphy shoes, and it can go barefoot.

Nothing can compare with love.

Yet, human love is but a shadow of God's love.

God is love. He is without peer. He is without comparison.

Bigger than any universe, richer than any mineral, warmer than any sun, God's love is greater than all.

To know God's love experientially through the reality of Jesus Christ is to know the joy of heaven. Not to know it is to know the grief of hell. Where there is no love, there is neither grace nor mercy. That's hell.

God's Spirit sheds His love abroad in our hearts through our repenting of our sins, having faith in Christ, and believing completely in Him. By God's love we are a new man. In His love we have newness of life. Through His love, we love.

Nothing can separate us from the love of God when it is lived in us by the presence of God through the Person of His Spirit. We are umbilically tied to heaven. We are united in spirit.

Once we become one with God in Christ, He lives in us and we abide in Him. Our identification with Him is in answer to our Lord's prayer that the "world may know that thou hast sent me, and hast loved them."[1] Jesus Himself admitted that when we are in Him, and He abides in us, the Father loves us as much as He loves Christ.

First love is the only kind of love God knows.

He has no second, third, fourth or other love. Because He loves us with first love, He requires of us first love as well. When we are not producing fruits in our lives that are His fruits, resulting from our obedience to Him, which is the evidence of our love, He commands us to return to our first love, and we MUST regain it.

Thank God we never lose His love. He said so. He said that we have left it, not lost it, therefore it can be regained.

It is like joy. The "joy of the Lord" is our strength.[2] But when, through a besetting sin, that joy is blotted out by guilt, condemnation, depression or the results of the transgression — we haven't lost our salvation, only the joy of it.

After sinning with Bathsheba, David cried unto his God, "Restore unto me the joy of THY salvation."[3] He knew it was the Lord's salvation and His free gift. And, he knew that only the joy was gone from his salvation.

With restoration after repentance came the love, and with it the joy. Many think that when they have lost their joy, they have lost their salvation because the feeling is gone. No. They have lost the strength of their salvation when the joy is gone, and when the joy returns so does their strength. The way it returns is through true repentance which leads to restoration.

First love, with that reverential awe that constantly rejoices in the miracle of redeeming grace, makes the truth of salvation always fresh, alive and present.

God's love is first love, and it is also tough love.

God can be denied, mocked, ridiculed, slandered, lied about, ignored, or told He is dead, but His love remains constant and unchanging. No wonder His Word states that if He loved us enough when we were His enemies to offer up a sacrifice for our sins, now that we are part of the family *how much more* will He freely give us all things.

We don't have to convince God to give us anything.

It is His good pleasure to give us the Kingdom. "No good thing will he withhold from them that walk uprightly."[4]

God desires to give us everything we need, and we are to believe Him to supply all our needs. He delights in our faith and trust in Him.

Tough love is not hard, crass, cruel, heartless, demanding or mean. God's love is unconditional, but His promises are conditional. Tough love is setting the boundaries for us to live within for our own good.

Tough love is truth in love.

Satan lied about God.

He told Eve that God had set the boundary in the garden so that she and Adam would not be able to enjoy themselves to the full. He lied. That lie lives today in the hearts of everyone who thinks that godly restraint comes from a God Who is only trying to keep them from having a good time. Wrong.

God's boundaries are an evidence of the tough love that calls for peace, order and concern for those loved.

White lines down the middle of the highway are not an evidence that somebody at the highway department hates you. They are placed there as a boundary to keep motorists from hurt and harm through accidents. Without such restraint, there would be only chaos, confusion, and evil work from unbridled license to drive.

So, God in love gives us our guidelines. Then in compassionate concern He watches over us to make sure we obey them to our blessing. Not to obey brings a curse. God wants our blessing, prosperity, peace and to bring each of us to greatness.

"Others may, you cannot," is what God tells those who desire His greatness and excellence in their lives. It is the reason why you may chafe at the Holy Spirit's restraint in your life, keeping you from doing something that you see others doing with seeming impunity. But the restraint is there because God desires to give you more.

Mediocre men settle for good, which is the enemy of best.

Mediocre men could have more, but they settle for less.

God desires to give us more, to make us into the image of His own Son, and to make our manhood truly synonymous with Christlikeness.

When God works to perfect us by trying us with fire, burning away the impurities and bringing us through with greater strength than ever before, that is tough love in action.

God's conviction of sin in our lives is not for our hurt, but for our good. He reveals our sin to us so that we can confess it out of our lives, and so He can reveal more of Himself to us. It is really an act of love on His part. His desire for intimacy in relationship with us is His motive for our conviction.

A cherished brother was found to have been engaging in adultery while still pastoring his church. His comment to friends after losing his pastorate, and almost his family, was "I know God still loves me." Like David, in knowing God's love, he was able to press on to tomorrow.

God loves even the most wicked and vile of sinners. God's love is sure.

What that brother did was fail to keep the conditions of promise, and he lost so much because of it. But he recognized that God's love for him was and is unconditional. God's conditions for His promises are simple: "Pure religion and undefiled before God and the Father is this, To visit the fatherless and widows in their affliction, and to keep himself unspotted from the world."[5]

God's love centers in His will. It is His will to give. It is our will to give back, and also to receive the gift freely given. Receiving is as important as believing.

When we please God, we are actually working for our own highest good. Not by striving for our own good in selfishness do we obtain it, but it is in surrendering in obedience selflessly to God that our good comes. David said that God's blessings overtook him as he walked in obedience to God.

Love centers in the will.

Love is a constant.

Love has three evidences: selflessness, the desire for unity, and the desire to benefit the one loved.

These are absolutes. We can rest our lives on them.

God wills my good. God never stops working for my good. Or yours. Or the good of others. It is His nature. God is love.

Christianity is not a religion, but a relationship. That is why so many people miss it. They practice some teachings religiously, but without relationship.

Love cannot exist without relationship. It can only be manifested when there is an object to be loved. Relationship is personal. That is why salvation is personal.

Nothing impersonal can ever truly satisfy. Men who try to be satisfied with riches are deceived because riches can never satisfy completely. There is never enough.

Creeds, philosophic forms or religious ceremonies can never save a soul. Salvation must be personal. Only a personal Savior can satisfy the soul.

Jesus is a personal Savior Who loves with a personal love. All that we ever need, desire or want can be found in the Lord Jesus Christ, and He always satisfies fully. People who have come to know the Lord personally have been immersed into His Body through faith by the Spirit. They have the revelation of truth flowing from the Word of God into their lives constantly. They are different from all others in the world.

God does not love us because we are good or better than anyone else. He loves us because He is love.

Some men are more intimidated by three little words than by the fiercest battle, the strongest competitor, the biggest hurdle or the longest marathon. They try to deny them, ward them off, or regard them as unimportant.

There is nothing weak or wimpy about saying, "I LOVE YOU."

Those words need to be said — to God, to others — again and again. Men who are truly men are not ashamed of the reality of true love, neither are they embarrassed to admit love or to express it. They show it in word, gesture, and spirit.

Men who try to satisfy their wives with impersonal gifts rather than through a personal loving relationship will always have trouble. Nothing impersonal can ever substitute for personal love.

Nothing is stronger than love.

God is love. Nothing is stronger than God.

Hate, fear, and greed are three powerful motives in human life, but there is one more powerful.

LOVE.

19
DO IT!

When was the last time you took your wife away for a weekend just to be together? No children. No job. No nothing. Just the two of you. Talking, loving, sharing, just being "one."

In marriage, a sense of "oneness" is vitally important. Without it, marriage can become a continual armed conflict — or worse — it can end in divorce.

Notice the price the man who wrote the following letter ended up paying because he was just too stubborn and hardheaded to change:

"I met her in New York in August, 1952. She was tall, attractive, and well-dressed in a gray tailored suit that showed off her beautiful legs. We talked of Los Angeles, both of us having returned from there. She wrote down her phone number on a cardboard coaster.

"I called, we dated, I met her family, and in October, 1953, we married. Oh, how happy I was.

"It went along well for a number of years. Our love was deep and wondrous. But I was unable to say that. Something wouldn't let me. I tried to show it in many ways. Gifts, a desire to please in all ways, and lovemaking in which I tried to let her know that all of me was hers. Still, I couldn't get out the words. I thought she understood that it was difficult for me, and that my actions would suffice.

"In 1954, we moved to Los Angeles, still very much in love, and were blessed with a daughter. Then, it started to go wrong. We couldn't seem to communicate, or agree.

We had our good times, our bad times, but always inside me was that strong undying love that I didn't express, but that seemed to hold us together.

"In 1956, another daughter was born, and in 1959, another. Yet we seemed to be coming apart. Why? How could it happen? Why were two people so much in love with each other, so much in need of one another, destroying one another? I wish I'd known then what I know now.

"Years passed, each of us trying to hurt the other more, each trying to top the other in retaliation. Yet, the love was still there, trying to break through the wall each of us had built as a defense mechanism around ourselves.

"Finally, it happened. In June 1983, she mentioned divorce. Not really seriously, but only a thought, perhaps, to open my eyes. At that, I decided to show her who was boss, who was strongest, who needed who the most. I filed for divorce.

"She asked me many times to call it off, but my false pride would not allow it. My stupid obstinacy, my great machismo would not let me back down. I would look weak and small in her eyes. After all, I was the strong one, the tough one who couldn't speak of love.

"I would go through with it. Life would be wonderful. I would really live it up, have many dates, and never have to say 'I love you.'

"Well, the divorce is final. She's in another city. There is no more pride, no more stubbornness, no more macho, and for me — no more happiness. I am devastated, lonely, miserable. There are no fancy women, no good times, just sadness to live with because I have thrown away the only one in the world who means anything to me, the one who made it all worthwhile. If she'd give me the chance once more to say 'I love you,' I'd never stop telling her that. After more than 30 years of having all that a man could ask for, in my own foolishness I have thrown it away and become

162

a tired, beaten, unhappy, lonely old man. I guess you could say I loved not wisely, and certainly not too well.

"I say, if you love each other, say it, time and time again. Don't lose what I did. Fight to save it. It's worthwhile."[1]

Amen!

Divorce is never the answer.

Neither is continual armed conflict.

I say "armed" conflict because the husband and the wife each has a weapon which they use to try to gain power or dominion over the other. In any contest between men and women, men often use their money, while women often use their sex. Many times this recourse to weapons is the result of influence from the parents whose treatment of their offspring exercises a power over them even after they have married and moved out on their own.

Ray and Meredith are an example of such a couple. She wrote to me about their situation:

"My father-in-law was always the minister's best buddy. He dragged his ten-year-old son down the aisle by the ear because he was 'embarrassed' that boy hadn't made a 'decision.' In his spare time, he jumped from job to job and town to town, tended to use a ball bat on his kids when he was upset, and literally terrorized his wife into a breakdown. When my husband was in his teens, his mother finally got a divorce; as the only child left at home, he assumed responsibility for her.

"When we married, Ray was in his middle twenties, and I was just over twenty-one. He was still supporting his mother. I came from a mother-dominated family, and had taken a job away from home just to get away. We were both shy, insecure, emotional 'basket cases' — and we had known each other only a short time before marrying. It wasn't long until we had serious problems.

163

"Ray was very deliberate, super-sensitive to criticism, stubborn and very much under the influence of his pastor. When we had a family decision to make, he would discuss it with his pastor, then come home and tell me how it was going to be. I was used to the woman running the household, impulsive emotionally, quick at decisions, just as stubborn, and not about to take orders.

"Ray had become a Christian and this pastor had drummed 'head of the household' into him to the point where he supervised the amount of water for my shower, and rearranged my kitchen cabinets. I thought that submission was only for women who weren't smart enough to learn their own way and stand up for themselves.

"I also made more than Ray, and bitterly resented turning over my check with no say in how it was spent. In two years, we were on the verge of divorce. I think we were too stubborn to admit defeat.

"Thanks to some timely Christian counseling, we stayed together. Things limped along for several years, with Ray's outbursts of sarcasm alternating with days of sulks, and my sobbing fits interspersed with equally stinging comments. I felt that I couldn't do anything to please him, and he thought I was defying him, which made him push harder.

"We had children, bought a house — but still were missing the real closeness that we both wanted.

"Then when Ray told me one night he was going to one of your meetings, Mr. Cole, I was unhappy, because I thought it would be just one more thing that he wouldn't share with me. Thank God, I kept my mouth closed and agreed to his going. He came home a different man.

"He told me he was sorry for hurting me — the first time in seven years. He sat down and really talked to me. He told me he was proud of me and grateful that I had quit teaching to be a full-time mother. Suddenly it was easy to 'submit.' I knew that I could trust him, and I began looking for ways to support him rather than fight him.

"We began talking and praying together about our big and little decisions. We also began to pray for each other before he left for work. Today, we are one. We are still different personalities, but now we appreciate and compliment each other rather than colliding and getting wounded.

"I am so proud of my husband. He has become an outstanding leader and priest in our home, and he is a terrific father to our children. His gentleness, love and support brighten each day for me."

The influence of both parents almost ruined Ray and Meredith's marriage. Ray used his authority with money to hold power, and Meredith tried to use her sex. They were both losers, destroying their marriage and family, until Ray admitted he needed to change — and did something about it. His change allowed Meredith to change.

When Ray began to communicate — talking with his wife, showing by gesture that he meant what he said, and proving it in his spirit with repentance and forgiveness — it changed their lives.

Praying together produced an intimacy that had been missing in their marriage relationship.

Some men wait too late to say, "I love you." Some never say it at all.

Some men wait too late to change. Some never do change.

If you want to save your marriage and your family, don't take a chance on waiting too late.

Today is the day. Now is the time.

Whatever you need to say, say it!

Whatever you need to do, do it!

ENDNOTES

Chapter 3:

[1]Luke 4:14
[2]John 14:21
[3]John 4:24

Chapter 4:

[1]2 Timothy 4:2
[2]Hebrews 1:3
[3]John 1:1
[4]Isaiah 59:14
[5]Acts 2:40
[6]1 Peter 2:9
[7]Matthew 12:36
[8]Proverbs 26:2
[9]Romans 8:1
[10]Proverbs 6:1-5 TLB
[11]Psalm 15:4
[12]Proverbs 18:21

Chapter 5:

[1]Psalm 84:11
[2]John 17:21
[3]John 1:12
[4]Proverbs 14:26 TLB
[5]John 6:63
[6]3 John 4

Chapter 6:

[1]Proverbs 13:17 TLB

Chapter 7:

[1]Matthew 7:21
[2]James 2:20
[3]John 3:16

Chapter 8:

[1]John 21:15-17
[2]John 15:8
[3]2 Timothy 2:22
[4]Ephesians 5:25
[5]Matthew 12:34 TLB

Chapter 9:

[1]Malachi 2:7
[2]Romans 4:3

[3]Hebrews 9:22
[4]John 10:10
[5]Genesis 2:24
[6]Hebrews 13:4

Chapter 10:

[1]Deuteronomy 22:21
[2]Deuteronomy 22:21
[3]Proverbs 1:7
[4]Proverbs 1:7
[5]Acts 9:31
[6]Romans 12:1

Chapter 11:

[1]John 20:22,23

Chapter 12:

[1]Romans 14:23
[2]Hebrews 13:5

Chapter 13:

[1]Isaiah 9:6
[2]Joshua 5:2

Chapter 14:

[1]Acts 20:35
[2]Matthew 6:33
[3]Matthew 6:24
[4]Psalm 84:11
[5]Genesis 3:9
[6]Hebrews 12:16
[7]1 Timothy 6:10
[8]Psalm 1:1-3 NIV
[9]James 4:17

Chapter 15:

[1]Mark 12:44
[2]Proverbs 11:25
[3]2 John 1:9 TLB
[4]Proverbs 10:4
[5]Proverbs 18:9 TLB
[6]Amos 3:3
[7]Exodus 13:18
[8]Luke 12:32

Chapter 16:

[1]1 John 2:16
[2]Romans 13:8
[3]1 Timothy 6:6
[4]John 14:15 NKJV

Chapter 17:

[1]1 Corinthians 5:11 TLB
[2]Proverbs 14:15 TLB
[3]Colossians 3:16 AMP
[4]Proverbs 13:11 TLB
[5]2 Timothy 4:2
[6]Proverbs 13:17 TLB
[7]Joshua 1:2
[8]Romans 7:24
[9]Romans 7:25
[10]Proverbs 27:17 NIV
[11]1 John 4:18
[12]Proverbs 27:10 TLB
[13]Luke 16:9 AMP

Chapter 18:

[1]John 17:23
[2]Nehemiah 8:10
[3]Psalm 51:12
[4]Psalm 84:11
[5]James 1:27

Chapter 19:

[1]*Los Angeles Times*, ''Other Views: Words of Love Unsaid, Their Lives Parted,'' name withheld.

REFERENCES

The Amplified Bible, New Testament (AMP). Copyright © 1954, 1958, by The Lockman Foundation, La Habra, California.

The Holy Bible: New International Version (NIV). Copyright © 1978 by the New York International Bible Society. Used by permission of Zondervan Bible Publishers, Grand Rapids, Mighigan.

The Living Bible (TLB). Copyright © 1971 by Tyndale House Publishers, Wheaton, Illinois.

The New King James Version (NKJV). Executive editor — Robert H. Schuller, commentaries by Paul David Dunn. Copyright © 1984 by Thomas Nelson, Inc., Nashville, Tennessee.

The New Testament: An Expanded Translation (Wuest) by Kenneth S. Wuest. Copyright © 1961 by Wm. B. Eermans Publishing Co., Grand Rapids, Michigan.

About the Author

Edwin Louis Cole is the founder and president of the Christian Men's Network, the world's largest producer and distributor of books and materials for ministry to men.

With seven World Regional Offices serving sixty countries, CMN ministers to tens of thousands of men each month via videotape in hundreds of CMN Centers. In addition, Mr. Cole ministers personally through "Christian Men's Events," special seminars, and personal appearances worldwide.

The books he has authored have over two million copies in circulation in more than a dozen languages.

To contact the author write:
Edwin Louis Cole
P 0. Box 610588
Dallas, Texas 75261

BOOKS BY EDWIN LOUIS COLE

COURAGE
A Book For Champions

Maximized Manhood

Winners Are Not Those Who Never Fail
But Those Who Never Quit

The Potential Principle

On Becoming A Real Man

Strong Men in Tough Times

The Unique Woman
Co-Authored by Nancy Corbett Cole

BOOKS BY NANCY CORBETT COLE

Tapestry Of Life

Tapestry Of Life 2

Available from your local bookstore.

Honor Books
Tulsa, OK 74155

EDWIN LOUIS COLE
AUDIO TEACHING TAPES

AGREEMENT: THE PLACE OF POWER $20.00
(4 tapes)
A study of the principle in Matthew 18:19. (A-102)

RELEASED $10.00
(2 tapes)
Deals with deliverance, forgiveness, personal release from besetting sins, fear, and guilt. (A-107)

STRAIGHT TALK X-RATED $10.00
(2 tapes)
Deals with one of the most common sins in the Church and the world today — sexual sin. (A-104)

MAXIMIZED MANHOOD SEMINAR $20.00
(4 tapes)
Presents the life-changing principles of MAXIMIZED MANHOOD. (A-109)

POTENTIAL PRINCIPLE SEMINAR $20.00
(4 tapes)
Teaching on the plan God has for your success, based on the life of Joseph. (A-114)

FOR WOMEN ONLY $20.00
(4 tapes)
A provocative series that will help women understand themselves and become the godly women the Lord has called them to be. (A-111)

FOR PARENTS ONLY $10.00
(2 tapes)
Draws lessons from the life of Eli, concerning the responsibility God places on the man in the home, and warns of the tragic consequences for the whole family when the father neglects his God-given authority. (A-112)

LEADERSHIP   **$30.00**
(6 tapes)
> The complete teaching from breath mints to Biblical exegesis. Start right, stay right with your church, Bible study group, or children's class. (A-130)

COMMUNICATION, SEX AND MONEY   **$20.00**
(4 tapes)
> The three most common problems in a relationship between a man and a woman, whether single or married. (A-116)

PATTERNS AND PRINCIPLES   **$30.00**
(6 tapes)
> A series of vital Biblical truths taught under the anointing of a 40-day fast. (A-101)

Available from your local bookstore.

EDWIN LOUIS COLE
VIDEO AND FILM MINISTRY

MAXIMIZED MANHOOD SEMINAR (V-302) $80.00
(4 hours)
> A powerfully anointed seminar presenting the life-changing principles of MAXIMIZED MANHOOD.

A NEW AWAKENING (V-303) $80.00
(4 hours)
> An exciting presentation of the 1984 National Christian Men's Event held in Houston, Texas. Dr. Cole presents an anointed message on the "new awakening" occurring in America and around the world.

THE POTENTIAL PRINCIPLE SEMINAR (V-304) $80.00
(4 hours)
> This nationwide satellite broadcast presents God's plan for your success.

RELEASED (V-305) $25.00
(1 hour)
> The teaching that frees you from guilt, fear and strongholds of sin.

AGREEMENT: THE PLACE OF POWER $25.00
(1 hour)
> A concentrated hour of teaching on the principle of Matthew 18.

THE UNIQUE WOMAN $25.00
(1 hour)
> The purpose of women and man's responsibility in helping to fulfill it.

STRAIGHT TALK: X-RATED (V-308) $25.00
(1 hour)
> Sex — God made it good. Frank teaching FOR MEN with a challenge for moral excellence.

GLORY OF VIRGINITY (V-309)   **$25.00**
(1 hour)
  Sex is sacred — Sex is the physical sign of the covenant
  relationship in marriage.

Available from your local bookstore.

If you have never received Jesus Christ as your personal Lord and Savior, why not do it right now? Simply repeat this prayer with sincerity: "Lord Jesus, I believe that You are the Son of God. I believe that You became man and died on the cross for my sins. I believe that God raised You from the dead and made You the Savior of the world. I confess that I am a sinner and I ask You to forgive me, and to cleanse me of all my sins. I accept Your forgiveness, and I receive You as my Lord and Savior. In Jesus' name, I pray. Amen."

"...if you confess with your mouth, 'Jesus is Lord,' and believe in your heart that God raised him from the dead, you will be saved. For it is with your heart that you believe and are justified, and it is with your mouth that you confess and are saved....for, 'Everyone who calls on the name of the Lord will be saved.'"

Romans 10:9,10,13 NIV

"If we confess our sins, he is faithful and just and will forgive us our sins and purify us from all unrighteousness."

1 John 1:9 NIV